AN UNFINISHED SONG

AN UNFINISHED SONG

MRS. GHOSAL
SRIMATI SVARNA KUMARI DEVI

GYAN

Published by

Gyan Publishing House
5, Ansari Road
Daryaganj, New Delhi-110002
Phone: 011-47034999, 9811692060
E-mail: books@gyanbooks.com

Distribution Network
gyanbooks.com
India, USA, Canada, UK, Australia

ISBN: 978-93-7447-315-3 (PB)

First Published, 1914

2nd Impression 2026

Printed at: Gyan Press, Delhi.

AN UNFINISHED SONG

Authors: MRS. GHOSAL, SRIMATI SVARNA KUMARI DEVI

AN . . . . .
UNFINISHED
SONG . . .

MRS. GHOSAL.
(Srimati Svarna Kumari Devi.)

AN UNFINISHED SONG

By

Mrs. GHOSAL

(Srimati Svarna Kumari Devi)

Author of "The Fatal Garland," etc.

New York
THE MACMILLAN COMPANY

PREFACE

This is a story of life among the Reformed Party of Bengal, the members of which have to some extent adopted western customs. It shows the change that touch with Europe has brought upon the people of India, but in their inner nature the Hindus are still quite different from western races. The ideals and traits of character that it has taken thousands of years to form are not affected by a mere external change. This story, it is true, touches on one side of Indian life only, for in a small book it is difficult to depict many of the numerous phases of our Society; still I trust it will give the western reader some insight into the Hindu nature.

INTRODUCTION

THE author of this book, a high caste Indian lady, is one of the pioneers of the Woman movement in Bengal, indeed the wealthy Tagore family to which she belongs has done more to raise the standard of the Bengali than any other Indian family. Although brought up strictly on Zenana lines, educated behind the purdah, and married at a very youthful age, Mrs. Ghosal was encouraged both by her father and her husband to develop her unusual powers of mind and character. Her father, Devendra Nath Tagore, was the great religious reformer and founder of the Brahmo Somaj, a society which devotes itself to fostering and preserving all that is high and noble in the Vedic religion. From her father Mrs. Ghosal inherits her passionate love and admiration for her native land, her ardent desire to rouse it from its lethargy, to inspire it to progress, and to help it cast off the yoke of its debasing traditions.

One of her brothers, Rabindra Nath Tagore, is the foremost Indian poet of to-day, adored by his countrymen, and eulogised both in England and America, where his poems have been issued in translated form. Another brother, Dwijendra Nath, founded what is now one of the chief Bengali magazines, which he dedicated to Bharoti, the goddess of Learning; while her third brother, Satyendra Nath, after visiting

England, set himself to tear down the purdah, to remove from Indian women the many and tremendous disabilities under which they labour; he has been warmly supported by Mrs. Ghosal, who was one of the first Bengali ladies to mix freely in Society.

At a very early age Mrs. Ghosal, or, to call her by her beautiful Indian name, Srimati Svarna Kumari, which signifies the Maiden of Gold, showed unusual ability and force of character; before she was twenty she had published an anonymous novel which became an immediate success, and the revelation of its authorship caused a great sensation, as it was the first time an Indian woman had attempted such a feat. Soon after she took over from her brother the editorship of the magazine "Bharoti," thus becoming the first woman editor in India, and, except for a short interval when her two daughters took it in hand, she has conducted it ever since—a period of twenty-five years. Besides her editorial work she has produced novels and short stories, poems, dramas, farces, and popular scientific text books for use in schools. Several of her novels have been dramatised and her plays have been performed before enthusiastic audiences all over India.

Besides her literary and editorial work she interests herself in every movement that is set on foot to educate and raise her countrywomen, and has herself founded a Home for Indian widows, for the purpose of providing a refuge for those unfortunates whose relatives, now that old customs are losing ground, no longer feel bound to maintain them; this Home is directed by one of Mrs. Ghosal's daughters, while her other daughter founded and directs the "All

India Women's Society" for the education of Indian women. Mrs. Ghosal's son holds an important position in the I.C.S., and is now on a visit to England with his wife, the Princess Sukriri of Cooch Behar.

Now that her children are married Mrs. Ghosal lives alone in the great Ghosal house, which stands in its large and beautiful grounds, shaded by palm trees and cooled by fountains, on the outskirts of Calcutta. Only a few months ago she lost her beloved husband, her lifelong companion, who shared her convictions and encouraged her in her work. Since then, although she does not adhere to the strict rules of the Hindoo widow, she has withdrawn from Society. She feels that, for her, the joy of life is over. "We shall be reunited in our future births," she says, and this she awaits with calm conviction. She has laid aside her wonderfully embroidered saris with their gold borders; her magnificent necklaces and bracelets and the splendid jewels that used to fasten her saris on shoulder and breast and in her dark hair she has divided among her daughters and grandchildren, and she now appears clad in flowing garments of soft white silk. She is tall and stately, a veritable "grande dame," her face is noble and expressive of high intelligence, and her manner calm and perfectly dignified.

One day for her is very like another; she rises at a very early hour, and upon the great terrace in front of the house she recites her morning prayer as the sun rises, endeavouring to "merge her small entity in the great ocean of entities"; she prays to the Almighty, All Beneficent Power, that good may befall every creature, that wisdom and happiness may be the lot of every soul on its journey up from ignorance to light. Then she goes to the south verandah where, after drinking a glass of milk, she spends the early morning hours in literary work, revising, editing, correcting and writing. At eleven o'clock she has her daily bath, an important ceremonial in the life of an Indian lady, even her heavy luxuriant hair is washed every day. After a very simple meal she rests and reads the daily papers or a book. At four she has another cup of milk, and until seven she strolls in her beautiful garden, or receives visitors (or before her husband's death she would drive out in her car and pay visits), and soon after dinner she retires to rest. Although Mrs. Ghosal still wears the native dress and retains all the beauty and comfort that India has to offer her, she does not hesitate to introduce European conveniences into her house, and her wide drawing-room contains English chairs and tables. There she receives her friends with generous hospitality ; when they first arrive tea is handed to them in pretty Japanese cups, then a number of trays are brought in covered with small dishes containing innumerable delicacies : quaint little cakes, delicious sandwiches, fried rice, biscuits spread with hot cheese, salads, fruit creams and sherbets ; the hostess herself piles her visitors' plates till they pray her to desist, and finally finger bowls are handed round.

Mrs. Ghosal is a forerunner, a type of the future woman of India, now that education is becoming general. She has not wholly emerged from the seclusion of the purdah, there are still many relatives even in Calcutta whose feelings would be grievously hurt by total emancipation, with them she still keeps purdah, the change even in her enlightened family is going on slowly. Emancipation is not all gain, Mrs. Ghosal thinks; women behind the purdah lived such peaceful sheltered lives, nothing came near enough to hurt them except the sickness or death of their dear ones; anxieties passed them by, there was time for everything, no hurry, no striving to be "economically independent," and Mrs. Ghosal, with all her progressive ideas, still preserves the dignified tranquillity of the purdah nashin lady; brilliant as she is in the eyes of her countrymen, flattered as she has been, she never asserts herself nor gives an opinion unasked; and indeed the semi-purdah in which she lives has the great advantage that it affords her abundant opportunity for her literary work and study. Mrs. Ghosal has read and thought deeply; although she has never been to England she is greatly interested in everything English, and reads many English books; her favourite author is George Eliot, for whom she has a deep veneration.

This is the first time that a book of hers has been brought before the English public, and it should be of deep interest to all those who are concerned with the Woman question, for it presents a careful study of the Indian girl at this intensely interesting stage in the history of her development, and particularly of her attitude towards love and marriage; all that is best in the old traditions of her race still holds her fast, but she is reaching out eager hands for the freedom that will some day be hers.

E. M. Lang.

AN UNFINISHED SONG

CHAPTER I

" Man's love is of man's life a thing apart,
'Tis woman's whole existence."

HE who wrote the above lines was a great man. It seems wonderful that a man should have read the inner nature of woman so clearly as to become aware of this subtle fact. In my own life, I feel that every word of it is true. When I retrace the history of my life, as far back as memory carries me, I see that I have always loved; love and life have been so blended that they became one. And were this love ever taken from me, life would be worthless, a mere blank, my individuality lost.

What was my age when love first came? I do not know the day and year of my birth. We had no horoscope cast, my sister and I. Once I found among a pile of waste paper an old note-book of my father's in which the dates of these important events were recorded. I tore out the page containing the record and pasted it in the corner of my song book, but the book got lost in course of time as books will. A search was made for it, and all the books I had ever possessed were brought together. The very scribbling block on which I had first practised the art of writing in big letters, from right to left and from left to right, even this appeared, but the song book, the book that was wanted above all others, was never found. Men will smile when I tell them of this lack of knowledge; they will grow sceptical over my simplicity. But women know what a difficult thing it is for the female memory to retain mere numbers. Both days and years escape them in their flight. We have no trouble in guessing the right day of the week, because weeks are short and quick to recur. But when we are asked the exact date of some bygone event, I would not ask any one to place reliance on our statements. We remember days by events, and only those days interest us on which events took place in which we were concerned. Let me, for instance, recall my sister's marriage. Before my mind's eye appears a moonlight night in the month of Falgoon.* I still see the calm moon in the clear sky. I see a night made bright by the lights and the merriment of the bridal fête. But the full moon and the bridal song did not record numbers. Ask me not for the year, because years are to us only numbers, formless things following each other silently, and like a sage meditating on the Being without form or quality, so has the woman to stop and think and count backward and forward and backward again when she wants to trace the year in which a certain event occurred. But there is one thing the great God in His mercy has made impossible for her. She cannot, however hard she may try, count backward to the day of her birth. That event is happily shrouded in oblivion.

It is all a great riddle, a mystery—this birth of man. The constellations are busily at work at a certain moment to prepare a future for him, but he who is most concerned is oblivious to it all. So after all it is no fault of mine if I know not the year in which my life commenced. I seem to remember 1882 or 1883, but how far these figures are

* The first month of the Indian Spring, which begins from the middle of February.

exact I cannot tell. And after all is there really any one who is the loser by this uncertainty ? The loss is neither mine nor the reader's. If the want of knowledge of these three hundred and sixty-five days would shorten or lengthen a man's life to that extent, it would be a different matter. But as it is, man may forget time, but time will never forget man. My age will be the same whether I realise it or not, and it does not matter much to the reader if I am twenty instead of nineteen. Let me assume then that I am nineteen in order to settle the question finally. I am still a spinster. This may be a source of surprise to one who understands this land of ours ; but it is gradually changing, for are there not many maids unmarried in this advanced age who count as many years as I do ? And if a surprise it be I have a still greater in store for my readers. I, a Hindu maiden, knew love before I entered wedlock. I loved a man without even expecting him to become my husband.

I do not remember my mother ; I lost her in my infancy. But my father's devotion offered compensation, and I loved him with a fondness greater than which no child could bestow on its mother. It is often argued that filial and conjugal affection are feelings of a very different nature. But my impression has been just the reverse. Here again I may differ from my reader. What the lover is to youth the parents are to childhood—the object of worship and affection, the idol of the heart. It has always seemed to me that a parent is protector and lover blended in one. Towards both we are drawn by the same desire, to make the beloved a part of ourselves, to have complete possession. The disappointment is the same in each case when love is not reciprocated, and we feel an equal readiness to embrace pain and adversity in order to promote the happiness of the beloved.

I had a sister but we had become somewhat estranged from each other. She was four or five years older than I, and lived with our father's sister in Calcutta for her education. I loved my sister dearly, and was delighted whenever she came home on a visit, but if she took up too much of my father's attention, if she claimed his affection in too great a degree, I ceased to appreciate her. After dinner my father was in the habit of lying down to enjoy his "gur-

guri" (large hookah). In this quiet hour he would soon find his little girls on either side of him. When alone with him I used to consider it my special privilege to twine my arms round his neck. In this way I chatted with him, asking every evening anew the same question, "Whom do you love best?" to which he invariably replied that he loved both alike. But notwithstanding this I used to be quite certain in my mind that he loved me most. "Do you say this because you fear my sister will get angry?" I would question. This only made him smile and remain firm in his assertion.

I still remember the many ways in which I used to show my solicitude for him. If it was cold in winter, his warm clothing was insufficient to keep him warm, it required my little shawl to cover him and protect him from the cold. The punkah coolie could not do his duty in the summer, father would certainly be very uncomfortable unless I plied my little hand-fan to cool him. I remember I used to make cuts in the potatoes, and decorate them after my own fashion, so that they might please him when they were placed before him. Although I often cut my fingers during this performance I could not be induced to abstain from it. If the cook listened to my entreaties to let me put the salt into the curry, I thought how very palatable it now must be for father' If ever he had to hurry off to office without taking the betel I had prepared for him, I would go without food that day. My poor widowed aunt. who superintended our household used to be put to great difficulty because she could get no flowers for her worship; for with the early dawn I was in the garden gathering all the opened buds for father, and no one else dared to claim one.

I remember that I was ill once while my sister was at home on a visit, and she took upon herself the duty of gathering flowers and presenting them to my father. Oh, how this pained me; I suffered more from it than from my illness. If I became cross and naughty, nothing would make me behave better so quickly as the threat, "You will not be allowed to rest with your father after dinner to-night."

I was at most five years old at the time of which I am writing. My young life was inundated with love, and from it I have drawn the conclusion that love is ever the same, whether it be between parent and child, brother and sister or youth and maiden. It is born in affection towards the parent, then passing in its development through the stages of love for brothers and sisters, and the fondness of friendship, it finally finds its full expression in the passion of youth and maiden. Just as I am the same individual now that I was in my infancy although I have assumed a different appearance through the growth and expansion of body and mind, so love is the same, though it grows, expands and blossoms out from infantile affection into the passion of youth. It can then no longer be sustained by the limited ideas of childhood, it seeks another object to which to attach itself, and as it passes through the different stages the heart learns in the end to yearn after the supreme ideal. That woman is blessed who, having found her idol, surrenders herself in worship to him entirely. That man is blessed who, once installed in the shrine of a consecrated heart, dedicates himself to her and thus justifies the end of life. That love alone is true which, based on self-abnegation, endures in its fullness throughout all time.

Thus I love father much even now. I would gladly sacrifice myself to procure his happiness, but he is no longer the only object of my affection, aspiration, desire, worship and contemplation, my only source of happiness. My all-pervading, all-embracing love did not twine around him alone very long. While I was still a child a rival appeared to share it.

CHAPTER II

CHAPTER II

I HAVE not so far disclosed the name of the place where our family lives; it is in the district of Dacca. My father has a small estate, but his income is mainly derived from service under Government. As long as he could attend to this at home we were very comfortable, but when I was about 8 or 9 years old he was transferred to another place. I mentioned before that my sister lived with an aunt in Calcutta, but I had not so far ever lived apart from my father, nor could I have borne the separation. Father accordingly took me with him to his new district. Here the only sort of school was at the house of the Zemindar of the village for the education of the children of his family, but many of the children of the neighbourhood attended it as well, myself among them. This is a custom generally adopted in India in country districts. In this school I made many warm friendships, but the warmest of all was with *Chotu* (little one).

I did not learn his correct name. Possibly he was called Chotu because he was the youngest of the family, but it never occurred to me that he had another name. He was the nephew of Babu Krishna Mohan, in whose house the school was. The boy had lost his father and was therefore dependent upon his mother's brother. One reason for my friendship with Chotu was his superiority in age. He was the eldest of the pupils and might have been twelve or thirteen years old at the time. There is a strange fascination for children in one of superior age. He was the chief pupil of the schoolmaster, and that worthy used to lighten his labours by entrusting him with the duty of superintending the younger ones. The school was conducted in one of the outer apartments of Babu Krishna Mohan's house. It began at half-past seven in the morning and closed at ten. But the pupils were usually on the spot at half-past six, and found Chotu seated on one of the benches. The master did not appear as a rule until an hour after the school had opened, and it was Chotu who took charge of us in the meantime. He explained our lessons to us, wrote the alphabet into our copy books, distributed sweetmeats from a supply in his pocket, and spent the rest of his time getting his own lessons by heart, perhaps humming a song while he did so. This seemed to be a characteristic habit of his. At times we used to press him to sing louder for our benefit, but that would end the matter immediately. Only once we heard him distinctly sing a line or two or a song. It was one morning as we were about to enter the schoolroom. One of the little girls, the naughty one, Prabha, had an idea. "Listen," she said, "Chotu is singing. Let us wait and hear him awhile, and after we have learnt what he sings, we will tease him and sing the song before him."

A day or two before there had been a theatrical company from Calcutta at Babu Krishna Mohan's house on the occasion of his son's marriage. I went to their performance with my aunt, but, unfortunately, I slept through more than half of it. Once I was roused from my sleep by a tremendous noise and saw a Prince dressed in brocade stamping his foot upon the stage in a furious passion and flourishing a wooden sword. I was very frightened but fell asleep again. Later on my aunt woke me to see a number of houris suspended in the air, a scene that pleased me. I thought Chotu might have learned his song at this performance :—

> ". . . . Alas, we met
> When moon and stars had faded,
> Springtime had fled and flowers withered lay,
> Garland in hand through the dark night I awaited. . . ."

Having heard Chotu sing thus far we entered the room giggling and laughing at him. Later I regretted I had not listened to the song until it was finished, and looked through numbers of books of poems, but could never find it in print. But now poor Chotu had to endure his tormentors : "We heard you, you thought we would never hear you sing, but we have." Chotu was greatly abashed, but as for me I never forgot those lines, although I only heard them that once.

Chotu gave away sweetmeats, as I said before. They were not specially good, only what we got every day at home, but when received from his hand, they were like the sweet cakes at *horiloot* that are thrown broadcast among the people and are supposed to contain special merit.

Now these sweetmeats were supposed to be the reward of good conduct, but soon became the reverse in my case. If Chotu had occasion to chide me for any naughtiness my eyes filled with tears and my gaiety changed very suddenly. This seemed to be more than Chotu could bear, and contrary to all rules he would give me a much larger share of the coveted sweets, adding caresses to the bountiful gift. This unfortunately did not make a better girl of me. I do not know whether the sweets or the caresses were at fault, but certainly my caprices increased. I would give a wrong answer even when I knew my lesson well. If Chotu came to examine my writing I would spill a drop of ink on his hand and laugh outright at what I had done. If he explained a sum on the blackboard, I considered it a special joke to rub out the chalk and wipe it over him. If on these occasions he showed any annoyance, I invariably resorted to tears, but if he entered into the spirit of the thing and retorted with further pranks my merriment knew no bounds. The result of it all was that Chotu's position as a schoolmaster must have been wellnigh unbearable to him, for all the children gradually followed my example, and there used to be lively scenes in the little schoolroom.

My father no longer received the choicest

flowers, for one bunch was given to Chotu every day in return for his sweetmeats and kind treatment. When I questioned in my own little heart which afforded me the greater pleasure, the gift of flowers to father or to Chotu, I was unable to answer. If in the early morning I found a bud that specially pleased me, the thought of father and of Chotu entered my mind at the same moment. I was anxious to see Chotu every morning, but at dusk I waited as eagerly for my father's return. I seemed to love him most with whom I was for the time being. I became more emphatic in assuring my father how deeply I loved him, at which he was evidently amused, for he usually replied by saying,

"Do you really ?"

"Truly, father, I mean it."

Then my father would smile and kiss me. Now Chotu had never yet kissed me, so surely it was father who loved me most. Then why should I bestow so much affection upon Chotu ? For love expects love in return ; of this I was convinced even in my infancy, although no one had told me so.

Thus passed two years, years so happy and full of childish delights. Often in later life how I recalled those days when I studied with Chotu in the little country school. Ten years have passed since then. I have known the fiery passion of youth. Mighty joys and sorrows, ambitions and aspirations have come and gone, yet lingers still the memory of those days, the memory of the love of my early life, when such happiness was mine as I have never known since, because it was unmixed with any sorrow. But life has ever been a vast riddle to me.

After two years my father was again transferred, and about that time my sister's marriage took place.

CHAPTER III

CHAPTER III

I SAW Him first at my sister's house at a tennis party. My sister's husband is a barrister who took his degree in England. He has a small party at his house every week for tennis. *He*, too, has been abroad, and is distantly related to my brother-in-law.

So I met him and fell in love with him at first sight, I hear my credulous reader laughingly assert. No, not that, far from it. I am not recording a romance; we only became acquainted. I saw him look at me and smile, and then turning to my sister, he remarked in a low tone, "You are keeping a jewel concealed in a mine, and letting a lotus fade away in a wooden box."

My name is Mrinalini (Lotus), but they call me Moni (Jewel). I overheard his remark, and it jarred on me. My brother-in-law, however, took it up and gave a whole verse of poetry in reply :—

"Full many a gem of purest ray serene
The dark unfathomed caves of ocean bear.
Full many a flower is born to blush unseen,
And waste its sweetness on the desert air."

Brothers and sisters-in-law in this country have the time-honoured privilege of teasing and joking with one another as much as they like. But, alas for poor me! I was so shy, and so unequal a match for him, that all I could do was to smile pleasantly and grumble inwardly the whole time.

Then there was my sister's brother-in-law, who had taken his M.A. degree in Sanskrit and would not let the opportunity pass of showing off his learning. So he replied with a Sanskrit quotation. which meant that a jewel does not seek anyone, it has to be sought.

Everyone smiled, but I did not enjoy the joke at my expense, nor look with special favour upon the man who had occasioned it. However, this was before tennis began, and the feeling was modified later on. After play was over the guests assembled in the drawing-room, and *he* was asked to sing. He consented, and sang an English song. But my sister was not satisfied, and urged him to sing in Bengali. He made some objections and apologies, but finally yielded. But what was this? The song he sang was the same I had heard Chotu sing in the schoolroom of my childhood:

"Alas, we met
When moon and stars had faded,
Spring-time had fled and flowers
Withered lay."

But I heard it clearly now, no longer in the humming tone in which Chotu used to sing it. His voice blended with the notes of the piano and filled the house with sweet melody. I stood spellbound and listened like one in a trance. I drank in every word of the song as one parched with thirst will drink without breathing when at last he finds the spring he sought.

Alas, this is a world of disappointment, seldom here do we get what we long for in its entirety. Scarcely was the song begun when it was interrupted. A friend of the family, Mr. Mullick, entered the drawing-room, accompanied by his wife and daughter. Both the player and the singer left their places and joined in greeting the visitors. This formality ended, the singer was urged to finish his song, but he refused. Miss Mullick was reputed to be a good singer; every one, except me, urged her to sing, and she remained at the piano till the time came for us to break up shortly afterwards.

Miss Mullick, or Kusum as we called her,

had hardly any chance of entering a protest in her modest way. She sang, and the listeners were so charmed that they urged her to sing again and again.

The mellow harmony of Kusum's voice, however, was lost on me. I heard only one song and the music of that dwelt in my heart:

" Alas, we met
When moon and stars had faded,
Spring-time had fled and flowers
Withered lay."

The music ceased in time. The guests departed and the house was quiet once more. But the song that had entered my soul rang through me still, and even in my dream that night I heard it, and saw the schoolroom of my childhood once more, now filled, so it seemed, with the furniture of my sister's drawing room; a party of guests had assembled, and I thought I heard some one sing the same sweet song, not softly humming as of old, but singing with a full and manly voice, while his beautiful eyes were fixed on me in a loving look—

" Alas, we met
When moon and stars had faded,
Spring-time had fled and flowers
Withered lay."

The music of that song and the deep tenderness of those eyes fixed upon me sent a thrill of delight through me and I awoke and found it was dawn.

I wished to hear that song again and again. It seemed I had no other wish. On that account alone did I look forward to next week's tennis party. The day came, the guests assembled, but the singer of that song of mine was absent. This was a source of great disappointment to me. At the dinner table I ventured to enquire.

"Why has not Mr. Roy been here to-day?"

My sister reiterated my question. "I was thinking of the same thing," she said. "Why did not Mr. Roy come?"

This gave my brother-in-law a chance for a joke. "Indeed! Well, had he known he would be missed so much, he would surely have come. Shall I send for him?"

This was all lost on me. I was attracted to the singer, not to the man, and so I answered unabashed.

"Yes send for him, he sings well. I wish to hear him sing once more."

I had no motive other than to hear the song, but I soon saw that they had, for my sister replied eagerly, "Romanath has called several times, but we have never yet invited him to dine. We ought to do so." My brother-in-law agreed very readily. Mr. Roy was accordingly invited and came in due course.

When I saw him again, I was somewhat disappointed. I had seen him only once before, and his personality had not made a very lasting impression upon me. Meanwhile ten or twelve days had elapsed. During this time, my fancy had been busy. I had imagined him to be like the vision I had seen in my dream. Though I did not remember the features I saw in my dream vision, I recalled the deep and loving look.

The man I met at dinner was certainly handsome. He had finely cut aristocratic features, a well-shaped head with beautiful hair, and he wore a glossy jet black moustache, but his eyes—ah, there lay the difference! They had not that tender, fond expression I had seen in my dream. In his conversation, too, I searched in vain for the ideal. His humour seemed very forced. He paid many compliments which seemed uncalled for, jarring on a Hindu maiden's ears. It was, perhaps, my untrained taste that was at fault. For how could one who had so long been accustomed to the best English society show other than good manners?

In the course of conversation my sister enquired the reason of his absence from last week's tennis party.

He had accepted an invitation to the Mullicks that day, he explained.

"I had refused them so often," he continued, "that I had not the heart to do so again. Did you really expect me? If I had known that I would sooner have sacrificed a thousand Mullicks."

"I say, Romanath," broke in my brother-in-law, "don't get so very eloquent, it might make me jealous, you know."

"What songs had you after dinner?" my sister enquired. "Does not Miss Mullick sing well?"

Mr. Roy smiled as he replied,

"Yes—at least that is her reputation, the general belief. What a lovely colour, it suits your complexion beautifully."

The last remark applied to the colour I wore. My seat at the table was beside him, but no conversation of any importance passed between us. My brother-in-law conversed with him on political topics. He spoke to me at intervals, but we did not get far beyond questions and answers. "Could I sing?" "Did I read poetry?" "What poet was my favourite?" "How long did I expect to remain at my sister's?"

In return I expressed my admiration of his song, and most sincere I was when I expressed it. Possibly he was pleased, for he replied, "I do not know many Bengali songs, I see I must learn them now."

This was the only remark I heard him make that seemed agreeable to me; I thought he spoke sincerely then.

After dinner he sang again,

"Alas, we met
When moon and stars had faded,
Spring-time had fled and flowers withered lay.
Garland in hand through the dark night I awaited
The bridegroom who would come when all was bright and gay.
Then the house would be filled with fragrance and soft music,
And the mellow flute the tune of Sahana[1] would play."

The song was over, but to me it was unfinished, something was left out. I was charmed but not satisfied.

[1] The tune played at weddings.

He then approached me, as ever, with a compliment on his lips.

"I wish I were an artist, I would paint you as I see you now." This time I was not annoyed; he seemed no longer a stranger to me. Of a sudden the dream vision and he were blended into one. And I saw whom? Him or another?

CHAPTER IV

CHAPTER IV

I FELT like one mesmerised, and this condition was repeated every time he called at the house. When I received him, I was perfectly indifferent, even in conversation. I felt towards him as a mere acquaintance, but when he began to sing my whole nature changed. It was ever the same song, and that song was the enchantress. I resolved not to ask him to sing again, but when the time came I could not resist. The strange fascination of the song lay in its power to bring back to my memory the days of my childhood. It poured a flood of feeling over me that awoke the dormant emotions of the maiden, and ere the song was ended, it created a vortex in which I felt myself carried into the realm of the ideal, searching for something I knew and yet I knew not. I was lost in an intense longing; it seemed as if a god had taken possession of him who sang. Anon as I listened to the melody it broke the barriers of time until the past and the present were blended and the singer himself became identified with one I had known of old, until I felt as if I were walking in a trance.

Nor was the spell broken by his departure; I often remained in a partial stupor during the entire night. Waking or sleeping I could not banish that song from my heart. In a day or two, however, I usually managed to master myself, and when I met him again after a week or, perhaps, sooner, I was perfectly self-controlled. Still I was shy on receiving him, because I remembered the spell his music exercised over me. My condition became an enigma to me. As the sky assumes different colours before and after sunset, so did my whole nature change with the coming and disappearance of the effect that that song had over me.

Gradually, however, this condition became permanent, and I began to realise the thoughts of others. There was but one opinion, one influence around me—this man was to be my husband, and to the thoughts of those surrounding me I yielded as every maiden of Bengal would yield.

No Westerner can realise what a powerful influence matrimony has upon the life of a

Hindu woman. Her husband is the representation of the Divine on earth to her, the object of her worship. There can be no mistake whoever he may be ; he is the only one, and none other ever dare claim a thought in her mind. She has been trained in this conviction throughout the ages until it has moulded her nature and is in itself enough to awaken her love and foster it.

Wherever I went I heard this one theme. My girl friends joked me about him. Older people discussed the matter freely with my sister even in my presence. My sister and brother-in-law let no opportunity pass of expressing their joy at my future happiness, sometimes jokingly, sometimes in serious conversation. There was no ground for thinking even in my imagination that this marriage would not take place, especially since he himself strengthened the conviction from day to day. His visits became more frequent, his attentions more pronounced. That he had not so far proposed to me, seemed to me due to a desire on his part to understand my feeling towards him better.

Love creates love, there is no other power so potent. When the heart is not occupied with other aspirations, it can soon be won over to love. As long as he who woos is not repulsive to the maiden of his choice he has little difficulty in awaking sympathy in her heart, and sympathy will grow into love ere long. There is always the desire in the female breast to make another happy by self-abnegation, for love is woman's whole nature, its desires and aspirations are her life blood. This ideal may carry her to the very gates of Heaven or, alas, if it is misplaced, if it finds not the right support, it may drag woman very low, and when she sins, it is because she has loved too much, trusted too much and desired to sacrifice herself to her devotion.

He gradually became to me the perfect ideal realised. His manly bearing, his engaging manners, these won my heart. I became proud of the fact that one so wonderful should have chosen me as the object of his love. Nor did the period of uncertainty last long. The day came when he told me what was in his heart, the day to which I had learned to look forward with pleasing anticipations—but!

I was gathering flowers in the garden. It was evening, and just after a rain-shower.

The air was doubly refreshing, and the flowers more beautiful. The setting sun illuminated the western sky with crimson glory, and reflected its hues on the clouds and on the garden in which I stood. I tried to pluck a rose but pricked my fingers. Just then my attention was arrested by a carriage entering the compound. It was he, and he came near and secured the obstinate rose for me.

"For whom are you plucking these flowers?" he questioned softly.

Yes, for whom was I plucking these flowers? That question I had revolved in my own mind ever since I came into the garden. In my childhood I had gathered flowers, but there was no question about it then, they were for Chotu, but for whom were these? I could not give them to Mr. Roy, however hard I might try.

"For my sister" I faltered shyly. I heard him sigh and then he picked a rose, the most beautiful one to be seen, put it into my hand, and repeated a verse:—

"A lamp is lit in woman's eye,
That souls else lost on earth
Remember angels by."

I blushed and invited him to enter the house.

"Go first and I will follow you," was his reply. "Do you remember you have promised to sing to-night?"

We went upstairs. My brother-in-law had not returned home, and letting my sister know through a servant that Mr. Roy had come, I entered the drawing-room with him.

He urged me to take my place at the piano and sing. "Please do sing," he said, "the song I love, 'Oh, mellow night with moonlight softly shining.'"

But I decided since this was a song that appealed to the night, it might better be sung later in the evening. He left the matter to my choice, selecting, however, another of his favourites.

"Sing 'Sweet Bird of Beauty'; you know the poem, I suppose?"

And then he recited the words,

"To me there is but one place in the world,
    And that is where thou art;
    For wherever I may be,
My love doth find its way
    Into thy heart,
    As doth a bird
Into her secret nest.
    Then sit and sing,
    Sweet bird of beauty, sing."

I urged him in return to sing to me, I wished to hear it. He took no notice of my request, but replied,

"I like one of Shelley's poems greatly, you must have read it.

> 'We, are we not as notes of music are
> To one another though dissimilar?
> Such difference without discord as can make
> Those sweetest sounds in which all spirits shake,
> As trembling leaves in a continuous air?'"

I remained silent, but he spoke again. "I once thought," he continued, "that all good poems were more or less hollow, that they were devoid of truth and consisted of mere fantasies, but I have learned to feel that I was mistaken. How do they appeal to you?"

"I have not thought about them in that way. I read poems and like them. That is all I know."

"But," he argued, "unless you feel them to be true can you appreciate their beauty? In earlier days I used to be displeased with a love-story because it seemed to me untrue and impossible. I see differently now; I now understand that

> 'There are more things in heaven and earth, Horatio,
> Than are dreamt of in your philosophy.'"

I never would have thought that I would learn to realise all this in my own life."

Then he turned towards me with eyes filled with sorrow and softly whispered :—

"'To see her is to love her, and love but her forever.'

Must I speak more plainly still ?

'To see you is to love you,
And love but you forever.'"

He was interrupted by my brother-in-law, who entered the room just then in a gay mood.

"Hallo," he ejaculated, "how long have you been here ? Just winding up the game ? Final proposal in poetry, it seems. Hurrah, let me congratulate you."

Mr. Roy was somewhat abashed at this unexpected intrusion, but in a minute he was master of the situation.

"You are very late in returning this evening," he said calmly. "We were whiling away the time as best we could. By the by, did you win that murder-case of yours ? Did you get that poor fellow off ?"

To an advocate no subject is so welcome as a talk about his cases, and my brother-in-law forgot everything else at this question. The two discussed the case. Meanwhile I was like one in a dream. I tried to think. He had expressed his feelings for me,—was I happy now? The voice of my heart did not reply. Something displeased me, I knew not what, but I recalled my first meeting with him and remembered that I had experienced a similar feeling then. There was something in it that jarred upon me. I was surrounded by happiness, all was beauty; I did not deny that. I felt like one into whose cup of nectar a drop of poison has fallen. The light of my heart became suddenly dimmed, I knew not why. It dawned upon me that this was not what I had longed for, it was all so short of my expectations.

While I was absorbed in my thoughts and the others talked, the servant came in with two cards and announced the arrival of a client and a visitor. My brother-in-law took up the cards, and exclaimed, "The doctor, Binoy Kumar Chaudhury. Moni, go and call your sister. Show him in, Durwan."

I went, and hardly had I crossed the threshold when I heard the voice of the visitor. Curiosity got the better of me and I stopped to have a glance at him through the partially drawn curtains. My brother-in-law had already left the room to see his client, and the newcomer was left alone with my lover. It was thus that I overheard a most extraordinary conversation. The doctor spoke first.

"By the way, I met Miss K. just before leaving England. She seemed very anxious to know whether you had arrived safely and why you had not sent her the money for her passage out to India. You know her relatives will have nothing to do with her since her engagement to you. So the poor girl . . ."

I began to tremble, and it required a great effort to keep on my feet.

"Nonsense," replied Mr. Roy, "there never was a formal engagement. I thought that affair was a thing of the past. For goodness' sake don't start the subject here, my friends might consider me a villain if they heard of it."

"What else can you make yourself out to be ?" was the doctor's firm reply. "Do you consider it honourable conduct to forsake a young girl who trusted you ? Before God you were man and wife."

I do not know what happened after this. I fell fainting to the ground.

CHAPTER V

CHAPTER V

When I recovered consciousness, I saw a pair of tender eyes resting anxiously and lovingly upon me. Once again that strange enchantment took hold upon me when I confounded past and present, when the days of my childhood seemed so near, so real that I felt myself moving in the scenes of early days, surrounded by the love that then was mine. Ah, the look of tender love was there that I had seen in the eyes of my childhood's friend, that look for which in vain I had sought in the eyes of my lover. The delusion lasted a moment only, and I saw it was not he, but the doctor who was bending over me.

"Thank God, the danger is passed, she is saved," I heard him say.

My sister sat beside me. She looked like one who had undergone suffering and fatigue. Her voice was weak and nervous as she spoke. She held medicine to my lips and urged me to take it.

I could not realise the situation. "Why must I take medicine?" I questioned. "Am I ill?"

My brother-in-law replied, I saw he made an effort to be cheerful, "There is nothing the matter with you. It is not medicine we are offering you, only a little sherbet; do take it." And turning to the doctor he continued, "Romanath is anxious to see her, may he do so?"

"It would be better not to disturb her for a while," was the doctor's reply. "She requires sleep to recover her nerves. Let us retire. Her sister then may lull her to sleep. There is no necessity for my remaining here any longer. With your permission I will call and see her to-morrow morning."

"Certainly," replied my brother-in-law. "What should we have done if you had not been here to-day? I don't know how to thank you."

These last words were said as the doctor left the room. I was most uneasy in mind. Some feeling weighed me down like a heavy load, and finally found vent in a flood of tears. I knew not what came over me but my fond sister was there to comfort me, and against her loving heart I rested my weary head, asking the one question that occurred to me,

"Am I going mad, sister?"

Dear, kind sister, how tenderly she caressed me, how solicitous she was of my well-being.

"Do not talk, Moni, darling," she urged gently, "the doctor has recommended sleep. Rest quietly and you will fall asleep soon," and passing her hand tenderly over my head, she tried to soothe my excited nerves.

I endeavoured to be calm but could not check the flood of my tears. I could not understand the cause of my sadness. Why I wept I knew not, for I was conscious of neither pleasure nor pain yet I continued sobbing like a child. At last I fell asleep, fondled by my sister's loving hand. Throughout the entire night I was haunted by restless dreams, my sleep was not peaceful. I was like one lying in a trance. I was awake and yet the nightmare of weird dreams surrounded me. It seemed as if all the events of my life crowded into my brain at once and then left it as quickly, leaving behind a sensation of peculiar emptiness. I found myself talking to some one, who suddenly changed into another. Again, I was dressing to go visiting but could not finish my toilet. I went to secure a carriage, but could not find one. I began to walk and walk but reached no destination, or if I did reach it, I was confused about the house I was to enter. Thus the night was spent in a whirlpool of confused imaginings. Only towards morning I had a vivid dream and I remembered it on waking. I dreamt my marriage was being performed, and I looked wistfully at the bridegroom, but thought that it was not he for whom my soul had yearned. The thought seemed to break my heart, and I cast my eyes down. Then I saw his feet and instantly I realised that it was he after all. Suddenly a divine happiness flowed into my being and in my ecstasy I called out, "It is he, it is he." The sound of my own voice startled me, and I awoke. The day was already advanced and I felt relieved and stronger, notwithstanding the haunting nightmare. Still I was not myself, the illusion had not entirely departed.

I thought I heard again the conversation between the doctor and Mr. Roy, and the strange experience that I underwent made me imagine I was another being from what I had been yesterday, and that the conditions of yesterday had disappeared and to-day was another world. My heart was filled with disappointment ; still I knew not that anguish, that intolerable pain of which I have heard those tell who have had a similar experience. Nor was I carried away by that ideal faith that, however depraved he might be whom I was to wed, he was my husband now and forever, and that I must worship him, be the conditions what they might. Deceived by him whom I had trusted so intensely I felt as did the beggar saint Durbassa who, when asking the love-stricken Sakuntala for alms, was roused to anger because she noticed him not. Even so my pride was wounded, and I began to loathe the deceiver. My indignation turned upon myself as well. Why had I been so blind as to take a renegade for a god ? Still I felt a grim pleasure at being disillusioned, for now I knew him as he really was, and from this man my thought wandered to the other, whom only yesterday I had seen for the first time, the doctor, who had attended me while I was unconscious and the light of whose eyes had welcomed me back to life. I saw the difference between the two. I realised in the latter a strong and manly character that claimed respect from all with whom it came into touch.

Thus passed the day. I felt my strength returning gradually. After dusk my sister again sat beside me, and seeing me much improved she began to speak to me of my ailment, tenderly questioning me of the cause that had brought on yesterday's attack.

"You have not had an attack of hysteria for a long time" she began. "We thought you were cured. I am afraid you have stayed up late at night reading novels. Moni, will you never learn to take care of yourself? Really if you are indifferent as regards yourself, you ought to be careful for the sake of those who are so anxious about you."

I assured her I had not been at all careless.

"Why then, this sudden relapse? Oh, Moni, if I could tell you what anxiety we suffered yesterday! Oh, the terror that took hold of me when I found you lying in the corridor. I called out for help and the two visitors who were in the drawing-room came to the rescue. Fortunately the doctor was at hand; what would have happened otherwise I do not know. Oh, how pale and wretched poor Romanath looked. When we brought you into your own room—you know he could not very well come in to see you, because the doctor did not wish any disturbance—I was told he went home looking terribly sad and dejected."

My sister's expression of confidence in this man sounded like irony to me.

"Yes," I replied, "he may have been dejected, but there is another cause for it besides my illness. Sister, we have been sadly deceived. He is not an honest man, and now he has been found out. That is why he appeared dejected."

Again my eyes overflowed with tears, burning tears of anger. My sister became anxious.

"I do not understand what you mean, child. Did he tell you anything yesterday? Now do not weep, it will excite you, and you may get ill again. Try to be calm and tell me what has happened."

I then controlled myself and as calmly as I could I told my sister all I had heard while standing near the door. It made, however, no deep impression on her; she acted like one from whom a great anxiety had been suddenly removed, and with a sigh of relief she replied,

"Oh, is that all? I have been so nervous. I cannot describe to you the state of my anxiety."

This was more than I had expected of my sister. She surprised me disagreeably, and my reply was quick and fretful.

"What do you mean, sister? Are you taking this matter lightly? The man is engaged to be married to one and proposes marriage to another—is not this serious enough?"

My sister was not convinced. "You are taking entirely too serious a view of the matter," she said. "As for me I do not doubt in the least that he loves you. Don't worry yourself about that affair in England. Supposing there really was some talk of marriage between him and some one else, what is the use of fretting about it? He is not married, and you know very well that engagements are broken every day. Not long ago the marriage of my husband's cousin was broken off even after the betrothal ceremony had been performed. Then think of marriage between a Bengali and an English girl. Just realise the difference in their habits and customs. Two people may become infatuated and yield to their emotions on the impulse of the moment, but they certainly learn to regret their folly when they come to reason about the matter. If the object of marriage is the promotion of mutual happiness, then such a marriage as this would be a decided failure. Under such circumstances I consider it far wiser to break off an engagement than to yield to a foolish and mistaken sentiment. And remember the happiness of the girl in question was involved as well as his, and should he sacrifice her life?"

I had not the patience to listen further. "Are you quite certain," I interrupted, "that he did it out of solicitude for the girl? Do you not understand that she has given up everything for this man, that she trusts him, and is waiting to hear from him? In the meantime he deliberately breaks his troth and seeks the hand of another. Is this worthy of the dignity of manhood? I am really at a loss to understand how you can take such a calm view of the matter?"

"Let me explain to you my reason for this," was my sister's calm reply. "You know that English girls are notorious for priding themselves on being able to captivate the affections of men, and I really think the poor fellow fell a victim to one of them. We should pity him rather than condemn. I am quite certain if we question him about it, we shall get a satisfactory reply."

"Do you expect me to refer to the matter when I see him?"

"You will not have to, he will do it himself. If not, your brother-in-law and I will speak to him. It is but natural, since you are engaged to be married to him, that we should ask him for an explanation."

"The marriage has not been settled yet," I rejoined, "and I have no desire for it either."

My sister looked amazed and exclaimed, "Have you gone mad? You wish to break off the engagement for so slight a cause? Now don't get any foolish notions into your head. Don't you understand that you will be disgraced in Society if you do so? He is a man, to him a broken engagement does not mean much, but when I think of your fate, I grow very nervous. There will be so much gossip about you, I don't think we shall be able to marry you at all."

"What if I remain unmarried? I am not very anxious for wedlock."

"Now in the name of justice," my sister urged, "let me appeal to you not to take any foolish step. If you wilfully refuse to marry this man, will you not commit the very wrong of which you are accusing him? Will you not ruin the life of one who loves you, and that for a fancied reason?"

"Fancied reason!" I reiterated her words.

"Certainly, for I feel convinced if we once hear the facts of the matter explained by his own lips, we shall find that he was not so much at fault. At least wait until you hear what he has to say and then give him your final answer. Even a criminal is not convicted without a trial, and you are ready to pronounce judgment upon the man who loves you without giving him a chance to say a word in his defence. I am afraid you are hard-hearted."

I was silenced. I saw it was useless to try and make her understand what I felt. She looked upon it from a worldly point of view. In her matter-of-fact way she argued that similar occurrences take place daily in life, that a man is not perfect but liable to the failings of humanity in general. If woman raises her ideal of him too high she must be disillusioned, and as long as he has not committed any extraordinary offence there can be no reason for condemning him. But my midsummer night's dream had vanished, and vanished for ever. I no longer saw with the eyes of Titania, to whom the most ungainly object appeared beautiful. The bandage had dropped from my eyes, and I did not even once attempt to soothe my wounded heart with the thought that he must be mine whatever he might have done. I was perfectly willing to pardon him as a man, but he could no longer take the place of lover with me. That place must be filled by one inspired by loftier motives. Whatever might be the shortcomings of men in general, he whom I was to call husband must be above all that is small and unworthy in a man. This might appear like a fanciful illusion to a maturer mind, but the ideal being unblemished carried all the force of reality in my inexperienced heart. Nor was I satisfied to have my husband's love for one life only, I must feel in my own consciousness that he had been mine in lives of the past and would be mine again in lives to come. That at any time his life should not have been entirely mine, that his affections should ever have belonged to another—I could not tolerate the idea. In this respect I expected of man what man expects of woman. As a man wants undivided devotion from the woman he marries, as she is not allowed ever to give a thought to any man but him, so did I want my husband's whole existence to be mine.

I do not know whether anyone sympathises with me, whether I can make anyone understand what I felt. I might pardon him, I might even marry him if need be, but he could never now reach up to my ideal. Time was when I thought he could be enshrined in my soul as all I had dreamed of in man, but I saw now that I had been mistaken. Now that the enchantment was over, he had become to me a mutilated idol, which could no longer enter the sanctuary of my being; my whole life seemed wrecked. Perhaps there is in the world another who harbours such sentiment as mine, but I knew of none, hence I remained silent.

CHAPTER VI

CHAPTER VI

It turned out as my sister had foretold. He came and himself spoke of what had happened.

"You heard what the doctor told me, did you not, Moni?" For the first time he addressed me in the familiar way. Perhaps he felt it would be improper to address me with the respectful pronoun after his offer of marriage yesterday, or perhaps he considered it his lawful right to do so.

I replied by a nod.

He continued, "I am afraid you think I have done something very scandalous. I am very sorry, but the truth is there was nothing serious—it was only a flirtation, and that is a matter of everyday occurrence in England."

I felt indignant but suppressed my feeling and replied calmly,

"But from what I heard the doctor say it seems to have been exactly the reverse."

"Oh, that meddlesome fellow, he is

an out-and-out hypocrite. Anything about other people, and he makes a mountain out of a molehill."

I could conceal my indignation no longer. "If a man is a hypocrite because he champions the cause of a helpless, forsaken girl, then what name is to be applied to one who betrays the girl who trusted him? Is he to be styled a man of honour?"

I felt my words to be very trenchant, and I regretted them when I saw the effect they had upon him. He kept silent for a while. When he spoke again it was with firmness.

"I have not betrayed her. On the contrary I should have done so if I had married her. I could never have loved her."

"Then, why this engagement?"

"There was no formal betrothal, but, but—there was a mistake. However, the fault was not mine. I had not thought it necessary to speak to you on this subject, but since you have heard of it, in part anyway, it is perhaps better I should tell you all."

Needless to say what he told me of the English girl made her appear as one who had sinned greatly against the existing rules of Society. He spoke in his own defence. She had constantly sought him, had invited him repeatedly to her house, and acted like one afflicted if he did not go as often as she wished. If she went anywhere, she asked him to accompany her, and so forth. It would have been ungracious on his part to refuse her requests. In this way he fell into a trap, but as soon as he saw that she wished to marry him, he became less marked in his attentions towards her.

This was his side of the story, but it failed to have the intended impression upon me. I only pitied the unfortunate girl the more, nor did it increase my respect for her accuser.

"But why did you allow her to be deceived?" I observed. "What may have been a mere flirtation to you, was evidently to her the expression of deep-rooted feeling. Your amusement was her sorrow. Such being the case you were in duty bound to marry her."

"Do you hold that because a man makes a mistake in an unfortunate moment he should on that account ruin his whole life? If I had married her, I should not only have made my own life miserable, but would have dragged others down with me. Do you not understand that this marriage would have been a great blow to my parents and relatives? I should have been lost to my country for ever, and in the end what would she have gained, for whose sake all this sacrifice would have been incurred? Would her life not have been unhappy as well? Since I did not love her, I could not have made her happy. In the face of all this, do you still hold I should have married her?"

This argument seemed true, but there was one point still unexplained. "Why does she still expect to be married to you? You should at least have had a final explanation with her, and asked her to release you from your word."

"I thought I had given sufficient explanation, but if there is still any doubt in her mind, the news of my marriage will make her position clear to her."

How cruel those last words sounded, how extremely repugnant it all seemed to me. She loved him, she still hoped to be married to him, and now she was to realise the situation through the news of his marriage. Oh, what agony, what heart-burning would she not endure! What claim had I on him? Had she not loved him first, had he not been bound to her before he had seen me? Could I have the heart to ruin her life? These thoughts revolved in my mind and excited my nerves, and my feeling was in my voice when I spoke.

"I do not know whether you have acted rightly or otherwise. It is not for me to judge you, the great God will do that. But let me assure you I will not placc myself as a barrier in the way of the girl who loves you."

My words seemed to startle him, he stood like one struck dumb, he had evidently not expected this reply. It took him some time to master his agitation. I saw he struggled to suppress his anger as he spoke.

"You charge me with having practised deception. However that may be, I have certainly not deceived you. But you have deceived me, you have played with me, you never loved me, and yet you did everything to make me think so. If you had ever truly cared for me, you would not now wish to break off with me for so trivial a reason. You would rather pity me in my misery. Oh, my God, must I live to bear this?"

Then we remained silent, both he and I. The minutes wore by, but neither spoke. My sister came to our rescue. She entered the room and greeted Mr. Roy, which greeting having been returned he said,

"I have to go to the interior this evening in connection with a case. I may have to remain there for more than a week. I hope I shall hear from you."

He then rose and held out his hand to bid me farewell. Once more he spoke to me, his voice was low and sad, it was almost pitiable to hear him.

"I have no more to say. My life, my death, are both in your hands. Consider this before you act further."

With these words he left the room.

CHAPTER VII

F

CHAPTER VII

My sister's conviction that I would be reconciled after hearing his version of the story had thus proved untrue; the reverse was the case. The manner in which he spoke in extenuation of his guilt had only increased my disrespect for him. The mere fact that he had tried to explain away the whole incident as a mere flirtation caused feelings of the deepest resentment in my heart, and when he began to say unkind things about the doctor in order to disabuse himself, I considered him more unworthy than ever. When in the end he went so far as to assert that I had deceived him, that if I loved him I would gladly overlook so trivial a matter, his utterances had reached their climax, he was then adding insult to injury. Was it then my fault that he was not as good as he made himself out to be? My resentment now grew into anger.

Nevertheless, strong as was my feeling against him, there was still hope, for his final piteous appeal had not failed to leave its impression. A woman may be cruel in a moment when anger controls her, but she cannot resist the pleading of love, that melts her heart when nothing else will. This is the essential difference between woman and man, it is here that the Creator has marked her as being distinctly different from his stronger creature. His distressed mien, his passionate exhortations, these had spoken to me of a deep love, and the thought of that went to my heart; I felt the pang of his disappointment as keenly as he felt it himself. Now that he was gone I reflected on the whole painful scene with the deepest emotion; I began to doubt my own self. The very words that had before excited my anger began now to move me to pity. Was it then true after all? Had I deceived him? Had I made him think I loved him when in reality I did not? Had I taken his future into my hands, meting out to him either happiness or misery as it pleased me best?

I now became overpowered by remorse, I felt the deepest pity for him. My mind became filled with gloom and I sat speechless, motionless, brooding over the things I had heard or said. My sister came and looked at me with anxious gaze, she wanted to question me. Just then the servant announced the doctor's arrival. This diverted me. I felt myself becoming calm, and when he entered the room I felt happy.

After the usual greeting he apologised for not having been able to come earlier, and then inquired after the state of my health. My sister explained to him that I had slept well during the night, and that she considered me much better. She did not think I needed any more medicine.

The sun was penetrating through the western window, and shone upon the sofa on which I sat. He closed the window, sat down on a chair beside me and felt my pulse. Then addressing my sister, he said,

"She is not quite well yet, her pulse is still weak. Do not stop the tonic."

I did not like the tonic, it tasted bitter, and I did not waste a minute in expressing myself on the subject. I declared pettishly the tonic must be stopped, it did not suit my palate.

My brother-in-law, who had just entered the room, heard my declaration.

"Up in arms again?" he laughed. "With whom are you quarrelling now, with the doctor or with the medicine?" I became embarrassed, but was still fretful.

"If you will only taste this mixture once, you will understand my feeling," I retorted.

"If that will remove your petulance, I will gladly empty the whole phial," he replied, still laughing. "I say, doctor," he continued, "will any one still question the intellectual inferiority of woman in the face of proofs like this?'

"We do not understand you," said my sister. "Please explain yourself."

"Women will play the coquette with fate itself when they have no one else to play with. They seem to think they can melt its iron, inflexible force with mere appealing glances from pretty eyes while men will boldly undertake to fight fate."

"But if fate is so inflexible how can you reckon them wise who undertake to fight it?"

"Well said. I quite agree with you," exclaimed the doctor.

"So you are taking their side. Well, I can't stay here any longer. I must go downstairs, I have a client waiting for me. See you as you go." And my brother-in-law departed.

The doctor turned to me with the consoling offer to give me a more palatable tonic if the present one was too bitter.

It was the expression of true sympathy, it touched my heart, and I know I expressed my feeling in my eyes as I looked at him.

What a little thing a kind word is, and yet the miracles that it can work. If men would realise what a heaven they might create for themselves by regarding the little things that women cherish let them learn to heed her wishes in all small matters! A woman can forgive almost anything for a word of sympathy, but withhold that, and there is no telling what he may prepare for himself, from coldness to estrangement, and finally a life of misery; this is the result, the daily result, of lives in which woman's nature is not understood.

In a corner of the room was a table with writing material. The doctor wrote out a new prescription there, and handed it to my sister, remarking as he did so, "I suppose there is no further necessity for my coming?"

"She seems to be quite well," my sister replied; "if she has no relapse I think she will be able to get on by herself now."

I did not like my sister's reply. She might, it seemed to me, as a matter of courtesy, have asked him to call occasionally. I felt annoyed with her, but tried not to let her notice it. The doctor started to leave the room, but before doing so, brought a small table on which stood a flower vase containing a bouquet of sweet-scented flowers and placed it near the couch on which I rested.

"The fragrance of flowers is good for the nervous system," he said, and bidding me good-bye, left the room.

How strange it was these flowers brought back the memory of my childhood, and once more I saw that school-room and its sunny hours which cast ever anew a halo over the memory of early days. I remembered how fond Chotu had been of the flowers I had brought him, how carefully he had arranged them in a broken drinking glass, and placed them on a table near his seat; how I used to bend over from my seat to inhale their fragrance and in my childish way exclaim, "How very sweet these flowers are. How is it that the flowers at home are not half so sweet?"

How Chotu used to smile at me then and look so proud and happy. To-day it seemed as if it were Chotu who placed these flowers beside me. I forgot myself in the thought of the past, and was about to ask the question, "Are you Chotu?" but the illusion vanished as quickly as it came, and ere I could speak he had crossed the room. A new realisation took hold of me. Was I going to love this man? I compared the weird fascination that Mr. Roy's song had had upon me with the feeling that now entered my heart, but I dared not yield. How could I be so capricious, so base indeed, as to forsake the man whom only a few days ago I had loved? Could I forget him who had vowed to me fidelity unto death for one whom I had never seen before, one who had come into my life only yesterday? Was it then true after all that I had never loved him, that I was deceiving him? If I had truly cared for him this incident in his life would have filled me with sorrow, with wounded pride, perhaps, but certainly never with anger, much less with the thought of forsaking him.

Yes, I had been wrong. I now thought I saw the truth clearly. I saw my fault, and my heart was filled with penitence. If I had been annoyed a while ago because my sister did not invite the doctor to come to the house again, I now was pleased because she had not done so. The man who had told me he loved me was to be my husband, and none other. I had wronged him greatly, but I would not deceive him. I would explain to him all that was in my heart, and if he wanted to marry me still I would be his. There would of course be no question on that point. He loved me with unswerving devotion ; he had himself said so. However unworthy I might be, he was too great, too noble to change ; he would, indeed, save me from the great error I had been about to commit.

Therefore, when my sister enquired about the conversation we had had together, I replied that I was firm in my determination to marry him.

" I have understood," I continued, " that he has done no wrong in not marrying her."

" Do you also understand how deeply he loves you ? "

" Yes, I understand it all now."

" Then you will have no further objections ? "

" None."

My sister was greatly pleased with my reply and consoled herself with the thought that he would be back again in a week.

CHAPTER VIII

CHAPTER VIII

I RECEIVED a letter in due time, a letter that breathed love and humility. It melted my heart and made me still more repentant. Needless to say the letter was written in English. That the love letters of a Bengali youth, whose whole life is one great imitation, should be written in his native tongue,—this preposterous idea would not occur to any one.

Of course, I began to write the reply in English. I was reputed to be well grounded in that language. I had received my education at one of the best English schools in Calcutta. My correspondence was conducted almost entirely in English ; the letter to my father and to my aunt were the only ones written in Bengali. I seldom even spoke in my mother tongue with my girl friends, and as to the English poems and novels that I had read, their number was legion. To tell the truth I was a little vain of the command I had acquired over the

English language, yet, however hard I might try, I could not make this letter a success. It was the first time in my life that I had attempted a letter of the kind. I positively found myself perspiring under the strain of this enormous task, and became terribly confused in the selection of synonyms and floundered about among adjectives and prepositions until I was half mad. I could not count the letters I wrote and destroyed immediately after. If the sentiment was fairly well expressed the language was not to my liking, and vice-versa, when the language was well chosen, the sentiment was not expressed as it should have been. Once or twice it really seemed as if language and sentiment agreed, but then it occurred to me that the thing read something like a novel, and I discarded it again. I became so morbid that a simple "in" or "to" upset me, and soon the poor letter lay again in shreds on the floor. Now could any one under the sun finish a letter at this rate? For the first time in my life I perceived the dignity and beauty of my mother tongue.

I had studied Bengali until my eleventh or twelfth year. Then I went to a girls' school, conducted by Catholic sisters who followed the Western system of education. So my knowledge of my native tongue had to a great extent been acquired by conversation. I had indeed read some poems and novels in Bengali, but of the higher classics written in this beautiful language I knew nothing. Nevertheless if I had had the good sense to write this letter in Bengali I should not have had to tax my brain so much about grammar and syntax. Strange as it may seem, we Bengalis do not mind an incorrect expression in our own language, but the slightest mistake in English causes us the greatest embarrassment. There is a saying that God is remembered only through difficulties. I realised this truth when I wrote that English letter. If we would bestow half the care on our own language that we do on an alien tongue we might carry its literary merit to the highest perfection.

Perhaps it was not the language alone that was at fault. There was that in my mental condition that was not conducive to calmness; when we have really nothing to say we can speak volumes, but when it comes to a matter in which our heart is involved, particularly when the affair is a complicated one, it is often difficult to find words to express our feelings. I wonder to this day when I think over the strange fate of this oft written and as often destroyed letter, whether it would have reached its destination if it had been written in Bengali instead of English. Who knows ?

The week that marked his absence was approaching its end, the day was near when he would return—and not a solitary letter had I written, although I had wasted a quire of paper in the attempt. I had at last abandoned my forlorn hope, consoling myself with the thought that I should soon see him again and that after all letters were a mere superfluity. It would be much better for me to tell him what I felt, I could never express all my feelings on paper. He would, of course, gladly forgive me when he heard of the tragic fate of the many letters I had written through the week, and so I rested at ease.

The week of his absence lengthened into a fortnight, and there was no news of his return.

But there was gossip, my sister heard of that at a dinner-party one evening. I saw her the next morning looking worried, and she asked me rather abruptly whether I had received any letter from him. I feared she would reprove me if she found I had not written. I therefore tried to evade her question.

"Did you have any music last evening?"

"No," she replied, "there was no good singer, Kusum and her people are still at Mymensing. Chanchal was there, she sang, but not well. I too made an attempt, but I was so worried I could not sing either."

"Why should you be worried at a dinner-party?"

"Do you know what the gossip is? People say that the engagement between you and Romanath has fallen through, and that he is to be married to Kusum. He is said to be stopping with them at Mymensing."

"Don't be depressed over a mere report," I said. "People have nothing better to do and so they gossip. Valmiki had finished the Ramayana before ever Ram was born. People have not all the genius of a Valmiki to write of great deeds, so they prattle about other people's affairs and tell stories which are seldom true."

"The report does not seem to be mere

gossip. I heard it from Chanchal's mother. She told me Kusum is to rèceive fifty thousand rupees as a dowry."

Chanchal's mother was Kusum's aunt, and the two sisters-in-law were not on friendly terms. They could not see each other's better qualities, and each found a considerable amount of satisfaction in finding fault with the other. This fact being known to me, I doubted the story.

"If she said it, you may rest assured there is not much truth in it."

"But I hear Romanath returned to town the day before yesterday. Why then has he not yet come to the house ? If all were well, why should he act as he does ?"

I had even then full faith in him ; even then his last piteous appeal rang in my ears ; I recalled the tender touch of his hand and the affectionate tone of his letter. My faith was not to be shaken by gossip or a day's delay on his part to come and see me. I spoke to my sister with gentle reproach.

"Didi, I am surprised at you. If he could not come yesterday he may come to-day. Why do you worry so much ? Only a few days ago you had such deep faith in him, and now you have lost it all through mere gossip. If his love is genuine this report cannot be true, and if it is not, then we have been saved from a dishonest man. I really do not see why we should grieve."

My sister said no more. But I received that moment as much comfort from my faith in his love as the devotee does from his faith in love Divine. It is an invaluable treasure, this faith. It awakens the heart to a greater bliss. It is because of the absence of faith that love is not always lasting, and often leaves the heart disconsolate.

CHAPTER IX

CHAPTER IX

My sister felt the effect of having retired late on the previous night, she therefore lay down to rest during the day. I was left alone and seated myself on an easy chair by the window, with a novel in my hand, but I could not fix my mind on my book; one's taste is subject to change. Only a year ago I was so fond of books of this kind that I stole time even from my studies for an occasional hour of novel reading. It had seemed to me then that I could spend my life happily with nothing else to do but read stories.

But now my book lay open before me, and I glanced through it mechanically, grasping of course not a word of it. I was, in fact, not reading at all. I was lonely at heart, yearning for something not within my reach, but what that something was I could not myself understand, and that made me the more lonely. I looked towards the sky and my eyes lost themselves in its measureless expanse. From it I turned again to my book. From afar the clock struck the hour. The sky attracted me again. Soft clouds appeared, and made me think of the sea, the restless, never quiet sea, that I had seen only once. I recalled a few lines I had once read somewhere, "There are places and times when the aspect of the sea is dangerous, fatal as is the gaze of woman." I remembered the simile impressed me as being most striking and beautiful. I had half forgotten it, but the look of the sky now revived its memory. I knew not the book in which I had read it, but the passage lived. If the sea is dangerous, then it must be an angry look that compares with it, but is a woman's look of anger ever awe-inspiring to man? Not being a man, I could not judge that, but I had to smile at the pusillanimity of man. I could not imagine such an angry look, such exasperation in a man as would discompose me. I am usually considered mild-natured, the sight of the least suffering in others moves me instantly, and for one I love I could sacrifice all my desires; but could another's anger tame me?

If on the day of our last meeting he had lost his temper, had threatened me, I should certainly not have felt any pity for him, nor would I have been so truly desirous of making amends. Love is far stronger in its workings than any other emotion. To me it could never be the angry look that would prove fatal, but the appealing glance that pleads for pity—this would find response in me, and this only. His tender farewell look came back into my mind. No, the sea is dangerous also in her sweeter moods. As the unsuspecting man who sleeps on the shore thinking himself safe from the distant wave is carried away softly, stealthily by the tide, so is the heart overpowered by the gentle melting glance; the man who sinks slowly into the embracing wave does not even wish to escape, and there lies the danger.

I heard footsteps; this startled me. I turned round and looking up saw Romanath standing before me. He was not smiling; serious, sad and afflicted, he offered his hand to me in silence, and sat down on a chair beside me. His coldness chilled me. He must feel hurt because he had received no letter from me, but how could I make an explanation to him while he was in this mood? I tried to speak but could not.

He broke the silence at last. "I hope you received my letter, Miss Mazumdar?" I noticed the change in the mode of address. His manner was distant, his language formal, cold and passionless. It almost froze the blood in my veins. The reply I gave was grave, and spoken in an unsteady voice.

"Yes, I received it. I did not reply because you were to return so soon."

"May I expect a reply now?"

I was prepared to speak to him. I had so long rehearsed what I was going to say. I knew it all by heart, but when I began to speak, I found how difficult it was to do so. I could remember neither the beginning nor the end of my prepared speech. It seemed as if the whole thing crowded into my brain at once and I became confused. I faltered a few indistinct words in reply. "I—what am I to say?—the fault was——"

"The same mood still—the same reply, 'The fault was mine,' you say." I had not meant it that way. I had meant to say the fault was not his but mine. He, however, gave me no chance to say more, but simply replied to my last words.

"Let the fault be mine, then; but can you marry me still knowing the fault to be mine? Do not think I speak from a selfish motive, think of what you will suffer if this engagement is broken. I have asked you to marry me, and as a man of honour I mean to keep my word. Do not be swayed by any considerations for me. Consider only yourself while you decide what course to follow."

The counsel sounded unselfish enough, but my whole nature revolted when I heard it. Had I condoned his shortcomings only to hear this? His language was careful and guarded, there was not a trace of sentiment in his speech. Was the report about him true after all? Had he been bought over by gold? My pride asserted itself, and when I spoke it was in a firm and clear voice.

"I am not calculating how much I may gain by this transaction. You need not trouble yourself on my account. I do not want to marry for convenience. Since your happiness no longer depends upon this marriage, I beg to be absolved from any further responsibility."

His voice was unsteady as he replied:—

"Then let it be so."

CHAPTER X

CHAPTER X

It was, of course, necessary for me to make an explanation to my sister, and this I did. I explained the situation to her just as it was, but if I had expected sympathy, I was mistaken. My sister was displeased, very displeased; she showed it in her voice when she spoke.

"I can well understand that there is gossip; no wonder he is reported to be engaged to some one else. You have brought it upon yourself, you alone. And all this has gone on secretly while I was thinking everything was made up between you. You may have had some abstract ideas of reconciliation, but how was the poor man to guess that? You told him plainly you would not marry him, and when he laid his case before you as one of life and death, you remained obstinately silent. When he wrote to you tenderly pleading, it did not suit you to send him a line in reply. What is one to think of such conduct? Do you take him to be a man without any pride or self-respect? It is a wonder to me that he ever came near the house again. The mere fact that he did call is in my estimation enough proof of his honour and goodness."

"That may be true, but the manner in which he solicited my final decision plainly proved that he had no love for me."

"I do not see that you reason correctly. However deep a man's love may be, if he sees it is not reciprocated, he will certainly act accordingly. A man's self-respect does not permit him to speak in familiar terms to his fiancée when he sees she no longer desires him."

"But when he calmly informed me to look upon the matter simply in connection with the advantage or disadvantage I might receive from it and put the question of sentiment aside entirely, what would you have had me say? Was I to cast all better feelings to the winds and complacently reply: 'It does not matter in the least whether you love me or not, I will marry you because this marriage will be my gain'?"

"But you had wronged him, you had hurt his feelings. If you had acknowledged your mistake in order to remove his uncertainty,

I do not really see how your self-respect would have been hurt. If, as you think, he adopted that indifferent way of speaking in order to extricate himself, even then you should have given him time to speak more plainly. As the matter stands he has been obliged to take the stand he has on account of your coldness. So far as I can see you alone are to blame."

I could not make my sister understand my action. According to her I had wantonly thrown away my only chance of happiness in life. The one object of a maiden's life is matrimony; she must be given to a desirable bridegroom, that is the goal of her existence. If she finds a worthy man who professes to love and is willing to marry her, she must consider that her future is assured, she has all that can make life dear. A husband's love truly is sufficient to counterbalance all the miseries that life can bring, but when that love is wanting what will constitute a woman's life?

My sister took the accepted view of the matter. Here was a desirable man who had offered to marry me, claimed to love me, would have made me a good husband; he was handsome and of good social standing;

all this was thrown aside by a foolish imaginary sentiment on the part of a girl who was incapable of judging for herself. She would not allow me to explain to her that he had cut me short when I would have come to an understanding with him. The cold, matter-of-fact way in which my sister reproached me touched me to the quick, it made my heart ache. I tried to forgive her on the ground that it was after all only her devotion and solicitude for me that made her turn so severely upon me. Affection expressed in this way has seldom a soothing effect. It took away from me even the power to reply, my voice became choked with tears, and I could say no more.

Scarcely had the altercation ceased, than my brother-in-law appeared with an open letter in his hand. There was both surprise and indignation in his face, and dropping the letter into my sister's lap he asked her to read it.

"What does this mean?" he enquired.

My sister read the note and then handed it to me. I found it was as I had expected. Here was a carefully worded letter containing a formal proposal to break off the engagement and explaining that it was by my desire matters had come to this. The writer asked to be exonerated from all blame and placed himself in as favourable a light as possible.

My brother-in-law took the matter as men usually do, he expressed his contempt for the man in strong language.

"He has broken this engagement to marry Miss Mullick," he said. "Upon my honour I will call him to account for this."

But my sister calmed him. "What he says is not untrue," she explained. "It is due to Moni that the engagement has been broken."

"What! this engagement has been broken by Moni? Is it still on account of that affair in England? You told me they had come to an understanding on that point. What has taken possession of her? Has she gone mad?"

"I thought myself the difference had been settled, but I now find that such was not the case."

"O frailty, thy name is woman. Why so much ado about nothing? This is the broadmindedness produced by your education, the fruit of liberty! What is to be done now? The thing will drive me mad."

I tried hard to bear up in silence under all that was said against me. That all this had happened through my fault was true enough, but would my brother-in-law as a man consider this fault of mine unpardonable if he understood the circumstances of the case? Would not the nobler sentiment appeal to him? I could not possibly lay the matter in detail before him as I had done before my sister, nevertheless I picked up courage and spoke, although my voice was trembling as I did so.

"What alternative had I? What answer could I give him when he told me to decide whether I would marry him or not simply out of consideration for the damage I might cause myself if I rejected his suit, and without any thought of sentiment? If he had spoken in a milder tone, if he had allowed any feeling in the matter, I should not have rejected him."

My brother-in-law frowned, and replied, "The whole thing appears to me absurd. I am at a loss to understand it. The man really told you to consider whether you might not cause yourself some injury before deciding what course to take?"

My sister evidently thought still further explanation was necessary.

"But you should hear the true circumstances of the case before you judge," she said. "He pleaded for forgiveness from her in a very contrite manner just before going away, but he did not elicit from her one word of hope. He wrote to her during his absence entreating her to take a reasonable view of the matter, but she would not reply. What could the man do after that? Is there not a limit to human patience? I think it would be better if you had a conversation with him, asking him what his intentions really are. If this is all due to mere misunderstanding between them, it should be put right."

The situation became most painful to me, tears filled my eyes as I pleaded with my sister.

"Sister, I beseech you, don't let there be any more said on the subject. Is this a commercial affair that we should barter over it? If he loves me, he will himself broach the subject to me again. Do tell your husband not to speak further to him."

My brother-in-law was walking up and down the room, he was in a very perturbed state of mind. Before my sister could reply to my appeal he spoke.

"I don't know what is the right thing to do. I am disgusted with the whole affair. Let us wait and see whether he says any more himself. On the other hand I will collect all the information I can get regarding him. I met the doctor yesterday, and asked him to come and play tennis to-morrow. We will question him about the engagement in England, and can then form a correct estimate of the man. In the meantime, however, it will be very disagreeable for me to enter the Bar-Library to-morrow."

"What grieves me most is the thought of father," was my sister's anxious remark.

Yes, poor father, I, too, was thinking of him, and there lay the most painful part of the whole affair.

CHAPTER XI

CHAPTER XI

ANXIETY, unhappiness, gloom on every side, my sister was grave and silent; my brother-in-law was fretful and vented his ire on the poor servants, who were terrified like hunted hares. It seemed as if even the trees and the flowers, the very doors and windows were bereft of their natural appearance. The whole atmosphere was surcharged with a frigid cheerlessness, and I was the cause of it all. The thought of it hung over me like a leaden weight. And on this day of all days my father's sister came to visit us, accompanied by her daughter, Promada. We put on as cheerful faces as we could, but try as hard as ever we might we could not wholly conceal the gloom. They evidently noticed it, and Promada bothered me with question after question. "What is the matter? What has happened? Why are you all so sad? Just because he has gone away for a few days? He will come back soon and then there will be a wedding. Can't you live without him for a day ?"

Times are not what once they were, the customs of our people are undergoing a marked change. Time was when each sorrow was carried to friends or relatives of one's own age and solace found by opening the heart to its very depths, but this is becoming a thing of the past. The young woman of to-day must learn to bear her sorrow alone, especially when an affair of the heart is involved. I therefore concealed my feeling before Promada and laughed her anxiety down.

The day wore on, and the tennis players came. A party of ten of us assembled in the garden. Although there was only one court, no inconvenience was felt, because the number of the players was not a large one. My aunt did not play, and I excused myself on the ground that I was not well. The doctor was there, and when not playing came and sat by me, speaking to me in his usual gentle way.

"You still appear weak," he said. "Your sister tells me you pay no attention to your health, you forget your meals when interested in your books."

"No," I assured him, "I have almost given up my studies."

Promada was by my side, and she took the opportunity to observe—

"I do not know whether she has left off her studies, but I can testify to it that she has left off her meals. Doctor, kindly give her a tonic."

"Gladly I will prescribe one this very day, but will she take it?"

While I was engaged in conversation, my eyes were on the play. When he asked this last question, however, I turned my head and smiled. He looked at me so gently, so tenderly, my whole being responded to the glance and the heaviness of my heart melted away in a happy sigh. The question involuntarily came to my lips:

"Have you a herb that will remove this weight upon my heart?" but it remained unspoken; I only suppressed the tears that mounted to my eyes and drooped my lashes. I heard my brother-in-law calling out:

"I say, doctor, come on, you are wanted to make up a new set."

He did not heed, but addressing me questioned:

"Has the tonic I gave you done you any good? How many days——"

"I say, come on," shouted my brother-in-law.

Chanchal came and said,

"Are you not coming? We are all waiting for you."

He started like one taken by surprise, hesitated a moment, and then replied, "Am I really making you all wait? It is too bad of me."

He joined the players. Promada remarked, "The doctor is a good man, is he not?"

I did not reply. I was in that happy, melancholy, dreamy state that all convalescents know, when body and mind alike have been wearied by illness and are once more being invigorated by returning health and cheered by the tender care of those who love them.

CHAPTER XII

CHAPTER XII

My brother-in-law invited the doctor to remain to dinner, and when my sister and I entered the drawing-room after finishing our household duties, we saw the doctor seated alone in a chair before a table on which lay a book I had been reading. When he saw us enter he rose, but my sister urged him to be seated again.

"What were you reading so attentively?" she asked. "*Middlemarch?* I hope we are not disturbing you."

The doctor resumed his seat after seeing us seated. He smiled, and bending slightly forward looked steadily at us. He was a handsome man, his features were of a fine and intellectual type. His complexion was delicate, slightly olive-coloured, and a soft glossy beard covered his chin and cheeks. A pair of gold-rimmed eye-glasses fastened by a gold chain enhanced his scholarly appearance.

"Pardon me," he replied gently, "whenever I find one of George Eliot's novels, I cannot help going through it, it is a great weakness of mine. I have read this very book several times, and still I thought I was reading a new book, I fancied myself discovering new truths. You have read it, no doubt?"

"I read it years ago," replied my sister. "It impressed me as being a good book, but there are too many long conversations in it. They oppressed my mind."

"That is true," replied the doctor. "They may be somewhat tedious, but the ideal of the author is grasped by them. Whenever I read George Eliot, I do not like to omit a single line. Whatever chapter, whatever page I may read, I feel my heart touched by a living sympathy. I am then aware of myself only as a spark in an ocean of consciousness, and am happy in drowning my individuality in the great sea of existence."

"I cannot quite accept your sentiment," replied my sister, "the heroine in *Middlemarch* married twice. Surely this is not a high ideal of self-sacrifice."

A gentle smile played round his lips, and passed away quickly. He answered softly,

"You forget, perhaps, that the moralist and the novelist are not the same person. The latter does indeed convey some moral lessons, but his main object is to portray life as he finds it, aiming ever at the ideal for which life should stand. It is for him to place before the public the different phases of human nature, the differences of character formed by circumstances, the influences of fate or the rules and laws of Society, all of which are again controlled by the laws of the Universe. George Eliot, who understands the mission of an author, does not want to change human nature, does not want to create either gods or demons. She only expresses life as she finds it, and awakens in her reader love and sympathy. Dorothea lives in the ideal, her hopes and aspirations are utopian, and yet what blunders do not such people often commit in this world of ours. This fact the writer has made plain in her character. Is there not a deep pathos in this failure of a life?"

"We pity her, but at the same time we must lose patience with her, because she loved such an unworthy man in the end."

"Some say," I remarked, "that Dorothea

and Maggie are but portraits of the author's own character."

"Yes," replied the doctor, "there is no doubt about it. As she was disappointed in her ideals and crossed in her highest hopes and aspirations——"

He could not finish as my brother-in-law entered.

"Why are you so late?" enquired my sister.

"I could not dismiss my client, however hard I tried. What is the discussion about. George Eliot? Oh, she is a great woman, we must admit that, I am sorry to say."

"That is a very reluctant admission. Do you not as a man glory in such a genius in woman? She had a truly grand intellect combined with the sympathetic heart and subtle instinct of a true woman. Think of the masterly way in which she shows that every act of man, small or great, springs from a deeper motive, a finer sense of the inner nature. Has any writer of the stronger sex been able to equal her in that?"

"I disagree with you," said my brother-in-law. "Do you mean to say she is as great as Shakespeare, for instance?"

"Of course," was the doctor's warm reply. "Why not? I have not the slightest hesitation in pronouncing her as great in her sphere as Shakespeare was in his."

This seemed to be too bold an assertion for my brother-in-law. He was half angry as he replied, "What a monstrous assertion; it sounds almost like blasphemy. I never heard such a ridiculous comparison. She is no more a Shakespeare than you are, my dear fellow, however cleverly she may have written her novels."

"No, she is not a Shakespeare, nor did I mean to indicate that she was. Perhaps I did not express myself clearly. What I meant to say was that George Eliot is as great in her own line as any author in England, dead or alive."

"That comes to about the same thing. However, prove it to me that she has as great a creative genius as Shakespeare."

"The burden of the proof lies with you, my friend."

To our great relief we heard the dinner bell ring, for my sister and I had become anxious about the outcome of this heated discussion. She therefore remarked smilingly,

"We might perhaps adjourn the controversy. We are being called to dinner."

The men followed our example in rising, but they did not give up their controversy, it clung to them like an evil spirit.

"You must back up your assertion by good reason, my dear fellow, or admit that George Eliot was not a Shakespeare," continued my brother-in-law.

"That I will gladly admit," laughed the doctor. "She was a woman, and although she called herself by a man's name, it did not necessarily follow that this made a man of her, whether it be a Shakespeare or any other."

My brother-in-law joined in the laugh and said, "The premises being granted the conclusion must follow as night follows day. Since, as you admit, she was not a Shakespeare her genius could not be on a par with his either. Now let us shake hands in the name of Shakespeare, the cause of our heated discussion, which seems, however, to have ended satisfactorily all round. Long live Shakespeare, the great man."

The doctor shook my brother-in-law's proffered hand and replied, "And long live George Eliot, the great woman."

"All right," was my brother-in-law's cheerful answer, "I have no further objections to make. Long live Shakespeare, long live George Eliot."

And they became hilarious and both shouted "Hurrah!"

"Are there no cheers for our own writers?" I asked.

"You are right," replied my sister, "why should we forget them? Honour to Bankim Chandra first of all!"

"Honour to every lady," put in my brother-in-law. "Honour to every man, three cheers for India."

And so the heated discussion ended happily, to every one's relief. My sister and I laughed, but our laughter was drowned in the chorus of their cheers.

CHAPTER XIII

CHAPTER XIII

THE controversy happily ended there. At table the conversation turned on lighter subjects: England and its icy winter, its skating and its snowballing.

"Don't you pity us?" said my sister, addressing the doctor. "We have never been out of this land, never seen snow or ice excepting once at Naini Tal."

"But the ice we saw there," I replied, "was not the same as you describe. It was a sort of a mound of ice, a mass of frozen snow collected in a gorge, where it remained unthawed even in summer. It was very beautiful, however. At one place at the base the ice had melted in such a way as to form a bridge, and the front having melted entirely, the whole had the appearance of a house, the melted part forming the entrance."

"It was a beautiful quiet place,' remarked my sister. "We reached it by using the sound of the cascade as our guide."

I recalled the scene to which my sister referred, and with my mind's eye beheld it once more in all its exquisite detail.

"Beautiful indeed," I exclaimed. "Nature is charming in that place. The abundant and varying vegetation, the hills, the springs, the streams and the ice—all these seem to have conspired to seek this lovely spot to avoid the rude gaze of man, and jealously diffuse their charms before Mother Nature alone. I thought fairyland lay stretched out before me when that gleaming white ice palace, those cosy foliage arbours and hills and valleys suddenly appeared before my view."

My sister took the occasion to compliment me.

"Moni describes well. I could not have made it half so interesting."

I blushed over this open compliment but said nothing.

My brother-in-law then turned to my sister and said,

"You are like myself, you have almost forgotten what you saw. Could you give any description?"

"Why should I forget?" she retorted,

"I haven't clients to bother me day and night."

"Well then, tell us how the ice looked."

"Oh, no doubt, I could do that, but am I here to be examined?"

"Very well, let me do it for you. Beautifully, faultlessly white, the sublimest, the beautifullest, the grandest."

My sister checked him.

"Now really, don't tease me any more," she said.

The doctor turned towards my brother-in-law.

"I see you are not satisfied with twenty-four hours a day, you want an extra half-hour or two. You monopolise the whole conversation."

"I beg your pardon," was the meek reply. "I will be as quiet as a mouse."

"That is good," said his wife. "Now you keep quiet and we will talk. The ice, well, it did not look like the ice we use in our drinking water. On the outer wall of the icehouse of which we are speaking it looked like frozen salt, and the inner wall was smooth and soft like wax, but it was somewhat blackish, having come into contact with the earth."

"Yes, and imagine," retorted my brother-in-law, quite forgetting his vow of silence, "the fancy took hold of these two to break some ice off the walls and carry it home."

"Well, you need not complain," was his wife's quick reply. "You did not help us in securing any, nor did we secure any for ourselves in the end—all we succeeded in getting were a few particles like dry salt."

"Had I been there," the doctor assured her, "I would not have left your desire unfulfilled. I would gladly have broken off a whole basketful of ice and carried it home for you."

"Now, my husband, learn from this gentleman how to please a lady."

"Ye gods, have I that still to learn? Have you forgotten how I used to make my fingers bleed plucking roses for you? That was before we were married, if you remember rightly."

She evidently did remember, for she blushed charmingly and faltered shyly,

"Well, well." Then turning to the doctor she continued, "Please do go on with your story. Really a river changed into a glazed mirror with beautiful creatures moving about upon it must be a fairy scene. I am afraid you became quite bewitched."

My brother-in-law was ready again.

"Became bewitched over what? The skates, the ice or the beautiful creatures?"

"Ah, but you were not asked," retorted my sister.

"Possibly I was bewitched," the doctor answered; "it would have been only natural if I had been, but the land had already charmed me so much, that I was prepared for any scene of beauty. The fiery, living liberty, the irrepressible energy impressed me first of all. There is not a sign there of the listlessness of our countrymen. One can do the work of ten men and enjoy doing it. Almost every student at my college found time for games besides being present at the lectures regularly, attending to his hospital duties and surgical operations, and staying up late into the night for study. Nor did they entirely absent themselves from dinner parties, balls, and theatres. I became simply speechless in my admiration of their energy."

"That is the great difference between England and India," remarked my brother-in-law.

The doctor continued,

"There is such a beautiful method of working there that one can accomplish a great deal without getting tired. Lives seem to move with the hands of the clock. Whether you go visiting or to meet anyone in business, you go about it as if you had to catch a train, time seems to be so strictly regarded. In the beginning this made me over anxious, and I was often half an hour ahead of the appointed time, lest I should be late, and so I would find myself loitering around the street to pass the time away."

I had been silent all along, but at last ventured to put in a word.

"Whenever I hear stories about England, I wish so much to go there."

"I think," replied the doctor, "all educated men and women should go there at least once. We are so moribund, it invigorates us to breathe the free air of liberty. There people are ever tearing down old institutions and building up new ones. Ideals which I dared not cherish here seemed to me there the legitimate object of aspiration. I became so bold in my fancies in that free land that I thought I could reform this country single-handed, could explode its deeply-rooted prejudices with gunpowder, so to speak. I now blush when I think of my wild dreams."

"God has incapacitated us," replied my brother-in-law, "there is no help for us. If the climate of India had been like that of England the history of our country might have been written differently."

"And we should have been born with fairer complexions," remarked my sister. "When our Aryan ancestors crossed the five rivers they are said to have been very fair. When I see the little English children with their soft white faces and cheeks like dolls, I can hardly turn my eyes from them. They seem to me like flowers in bloom. Why has not God made us fair like them?"

"You ought not to fret on that account," rejoined her husband. "Have we not proof of the fact that dark beauty conquered where all else failed?"

"But oh, fair beauty could have done much more."

"I do not agree with you," her husband replied. "What do you say, doctor? You have come back from that land of the sun, do you think you can remain unmoved in this land of beautiful moonlight? You see my plight?"

"But you can appreciate the moonlight better, after having been scorched by the sun. Otherwise I fear you would not have remembered your native land. It seems to me people become so fascinated that in a short time they forget country, relations and all. That is really a great surprise to me."

"But the wonder to me is that our Bengali youths do not forget their country altogether." It was my brother-in-law who spoke again. "That any of us return as bachelors and marry as soon as we come back in spite of the charms we leave behind, is the most marvellous part of all."

"Very well, you may return to England, nobody is preventing you," said my sister.

"Well, well, you are very generous indeed to make me this offer now that you see I am bound down by a chain."

I do not know how long this jest between husband and wife might have continued had I not interrupted it.

"Tell me what pleased you most in that land?" I asked the doctor.

"What pleased me most? The women's——"

"Beauty," broke in my brother-in-law. "Good heavens, man, I have never yet been guilty of that remark."

"It is very courteous of you, doctor," said my sister laughingly, "to tell us that to our face."

"But pardon, madame, it was not I who said that, it was your husband. What I liked best was the liberty and self-reliance of the women. Day by day their sphere of activity expands until they have begun to invade the realms of politics. The men may laugh at them, but nevertheless they respect their women for it. It is impossible for us to realise here what influence those women exercise on their country and on the individual, and how beneficent that influence is. Our life seems purposeless compared with it."

"But," I replied, "since in our country men and women mix together so little, it must seem very strange to a new comer to find himself constantly in the company of ladies."

"That is true. I must admit my condition was a miserable one. To give you a simile, I felt like one trying to keep afloat in the Ganges with only a thread to guide him to the opposite shore."

My sister laughed most cordially at this comparison and asked him to explain.

He continued, "I did not know the habits, manners and customs, nor yet the language properly. We learn the language by studying philosophy, history and science in books, but we cannot carry on a conversation in short sentences nor return an answer. When introduced to a lady I would become nervous and awkward. I had learned my words entirely from the dictionary and had laid the greatest stress on accent and pronunciation. The result was I could hardly understand English people when they spoke to me. There was still another difficulty. I was told again and again, 'You have cut So-and-So; he lifted his hat to you in the street but you did not return his greeting!' Good heavens! whom had I met, who had lifted his hat to me? My life was practically teased out of me by having to make excuses for this kind of thing every day. The fact was I did not look around me very much when walking, moreover those white faces looked to me so much alike that unless one was particularly familiar to me, it was difficult for me to recognise it. Again, if I entered a shop to make a purchase worth a penny, I found myself five pounds poorer when going over my cash account that evening, simply on account of the importunity of the shopkeeper. It is necessary to learn to say 'no' in that land, or there is no end of danger. I finally learned to stand erect on English soil, but Heaven alone knows how often I tripped before I accomplished it."

"At last you became master of the situation?" asked my sister.

"I cannot even say that, madame. My Bengali friends used to tell me I was hopelessly green up to the last."

"How long did you know Romanath there?" asked my brother-in-law.

"I met him at the house of a mutual friend only a few days before I left England."

"Was he really engaged to be married?"

The doctor looked taken aback. He hesitated for a while and then replied, "I heard so, but—I am afraid this is not a fit subject for the dinner table."

"You are right," replied my brother-in-law, "let us discuss the matter another time. I have my own reasons for asking you."

The subject was dropped accordingly, to my great relief.

The night that followed was one of exquisite moonlight, sky and earth alike were illumined by a silver glow. We repaired to the terrace after dinner.

My sister addressed the doctor, saying, "According to your account everything in England is superb; but had you ever there a moon like this?"

"Moonlight was rare indeed. Perhaps it was owing to this fact that it used to look so glorious when it did appear."

"You are hopelessly bewitched, I see," rejoined my sister. "Not only does England hold the most beautiful women, but the most perfect moon as well. How could you ever in the face of all these fascinations come back again? Really that puzzles me."

He caressed his handsome beard and smiled.

"Truth is sometimes stranger than fiction. When the chances are good, there is almost always disappointment, and where one expects the least, there often the unexpected happens."

As he said this he threw a timid glance at me. That glance and the moonlight seemed like harmony blended. A thrill of happiness went through my being and I sighed.

CHAPTER XIV

CHAPTER XIV

WHEN a visitor leaves he is usually discussed. So after the doctor had taken his leave, we spoke of him for a while.

"He makes a good impression," remarked my sister.

"Yes, he is not a bad fellow," rejoined my brother-in-law. "He has not much common sense, though, too much of a woman worshipper I should say."

"That is good."

"Who says it is bad? Poor fellow, I pity him. He is quite lost in admiration of the fair sex. Fancy, an intelligent young man believing in the possibility of a female Shakespeare."

"Is that such an impossible thing?"

"And what is worse still, he does not hesitate to make a fool of himself by expressing his outrageous opinion before others. I wonder if the man has any idea how ludicrous it sounds."

"It seems to me a proof of the fact that he has great strength of conviction." This remark came from me.

My brother-in-law turned towards me and said,

"You are right, it shows his sincerity. I like him the better for his outspoken foolish enthusiasm."

"The man has a warm heart," said my sister."

"Yes, and the manners of a perfect gentleman," replied her husband. Then as if a new idea took hold of him suddenly he exclaimed,

"How would you like to see him married to Moni?"

"He is already engaged," replied my sister.

"Good Gods, who has told you that? I thought he was rather—aw—well, never mind what I thought. But who told you that he is engaged?"

"Chanchal's mother told me."

"Who has tackled him so soon? The report may after all be mere gossip."

"No," replied my sister. "It does not seem to be that. She heard it from the doctor's mother, but who the chosen lady is I do not know. I did not enquire. What was the good of my knowing ? "

" Bad luck everywhere. Well, let's retire and congratulate the happy pair in our dreams."

It was fortunate for me that it was dark, they could not therefore see the sudden change in my face. I know I must have turned pale, I felt it.

Alone in my room that night I found no sleep. I sat by the open window and gazed into the beautiful moonlight before me. Clouds of varying hue passed softly over the sky. I reflected what this evening had brought to me. I saw one face ever before me, until the sorrow that filled my heart overflowed and filled my eyes with tears. Was it merely fancy after all ? That deep fond glance he had cast at me, the uncommon cordiality he showed even in ordinary conversation, were they after all no more than the expression of his own deep nature ? How little, how unworthy I suddenly appeared in my own eyes. How could I forget myself so far as to think that this was all for me ? No, it could never, never be, it was all a delusion, a fancy.

There was the moonlight outside and the light of those eyes in my heart, but the cheerfulness I had felt in his presence was gone and melancholy and dejection took its place, the spring that had entered my heart a few hours ago was already withering before the wintry blast of reality.

He, too, came back to my mind, the man whose love I had spurned. We are taught Karma, that is to say, the effect of causes created by ourselves. Had this sorrow come upon me because I had caused pain to another? Had I occasioned my own affliction? Be that as it might I could not bring back the love that I knew, and this new love had not come to me through any desire on my part. I would gladly have torn it from my heart for ever, for it gave me no happiness. Was it the uncontrollable force of Karma again that had brought this new passion into my life? If man is not responsible, then why must he suffer so? Oh, great Creator, behold Thy work, how helpless, how weak are thy creatures! Still into the darkness of this hour, I felt God's mercy shining, I thought of my childhood once more, and a pathetic prayer breathed from my heart:

"Oh, merciful God, even as Thou took pity upon me when I was a helpless child and gave peace and happiness to my young life, grant me to-day——"

The prayer died unfinished on my lips. What was I doing? Praying to God to give to me the lawful right of another? Another was to sacrifice her life's happiness for my sake? The feeling that came over me with this sudden change of thought overpowered me and I fell helplessly to the ground, and there in my agony I groaned another prayer:

"Mercy, Divine God, oh grant me strength to endure. Help me to bear up in patience under a trial which will but purify my life in the end. Have mercy, O Lord!" And thus amid prayers and tears I fell asleep that night, but the dawn brought no relief, the terrible experience of the night just passed was upon me still, and the vision of that face, that look so tender, followed me like a shadow.

CHAPTER XV

CHAPTER XV

I REMAINED in the same condition as the day wore on, aimless, without hope, without any desire even to fight the inevitable, yet as water struggles underneath a rock, so did the instinct of life work underneath despair, my emotions were at war with each other. I felt like one bleeding from a thousand wounds in this struggle with myself. I felt as if in God's Kingdom there was not another that suffered as I did.

And still the whole affair filled me with amazement at my own nature. I had known him only a few days, I had spoken to him a few times only. Was I then going mad that I should give way to my feelings in this way? I felt as if I could draw into my being at once all the beauty and sorrow, the joy and agony, the happiness and misery of all existence since that sacred moment when my soul touched his.

I had thought I loved the other, but oh,

how far short had been that feeling of what now controlled me. He had fascinated me with a song, had brought upon me the pain of past memories. What knew I then of this complete immolation of body and soul? That emotion had been but the outcome of a strong sympathy, a deep-rooted faith in love I had thought to be genuine, but when it had been unable to stand the test, the faith that had gone with it, and which I had mistaken for love, had died out. Now even though the feeling I had for this man brought me no happiness, nay worse, carried me to the every verge of despair itself, yet I had no desire to get away from it, it became on the contrary more firmly rooted in my being with every fleeting moment.

My daily duties became a thing apart from my life. People came and spoke of affairs, I spoke with them, but it all seemed like something far away, something in which I was no longer concerned. I endeavoured to forget him, but every endeavour brought nearer to me the consciousness of my great love. My being became composed of it, and whatever came into my life became converted into it. The very breezes whispered of a love that was mine, mine, and yet not mine. From out the vastness of space came a cry of despair, of agony.

"I ask not to be his," called out my feeble heart. "I ask but to see him, to hear his voice at times. Grant me that, oh Fate, and I shall feel compensated for the sorrow of existence." There was no wounded pride in this, I had no pride to wound, humility alone claimed me as her own.

Thus as the days went by the fire in my soul burnt on. I knew not whether time would bring peace, but it seemed to me there was but one flame that could extinguish the agony, the pain that would not leave me, and that was the last, the flame that consumes all that is mortal in man. Was I really to drag on this life until I was old? I shuddered at the very thought. Was this, then, the love I had dreamt of, was it to find its realisation in a yearning not to be satisfied, a groping for something that could not be grasped?

Chanchal came to see me one afternoon. She was my bosom friend. We were in the habit of spending one day together at least once a week. Her searching eyes noticed a change in me, the melancholy that was written on my face did not escape her.

"You say it has not affected you? It is too terrible to see how you look. I am so angry with him. And just think of it, my uncle and aunt proposed to marry my cousin to him." Chanchal became excited as she said this.

"I am very glad to hear it," I replied.

"Moni, do you mean that? Can you tell me in good faith that you do not love him any more, that you are not sorry because the engagement has been broken off?"

"I am not sorry. Chanchal, do you think I would tell you an untruth? I might not tell you all that is in my heart, but tell you a falsehood—never."

Chanchal was evidently delighted at this assurance. She pressed my cheeks between her palms and exclaimed:

"You dear, sweet friend, I do not know then what ails you. You are not in your best mood. Certainly you trusted this man, and he deceived you. That must cause you pain."

"Yes, it caused me some pain, that I will not deny, but do not think that I am pining over that affair now."

"If I had been in your place I should have died. If ever a week passes without a letter from England for me, I don't know what I am doing."

"Ah, but you are married. Even if your husband should forget you, you can never forget him, but my case was different; I could forget and I did."

"That may be the differencc. Cousin Kusum, too, is quite at ease. I see I introduced perhaps too much of my own feeling into the matter when sympathising with you. Have you heard that Kusum's engagement to Mr. Roy, too, has been broken off?"

"No, I have not heard of it. Why?"

"That I do not know. They do not disclose everything to us, but I hear from other people that the marriage will not take place. I believe it is Romanath who has broken it off, because I understood Kusum was willing. Really the man must have extraordinary powers, or never would he have been able to make an impression on cousin Kusum!"

This news affected me. I felt remorse again. Why should he have objected to this marriage? Was this on my account still ? Chanchal noticed my pensive mood and enquired,

" What are you thinking so earnestly ? "

" Did your cousin really love him ? " I asked Chancal. " My heart aches for her. Had I the power I would bring about the marriage."

" You ? You pity my cousin ? Would she waste so much sentiment on you ? There is no need to pity my cousin, she has sufficient self-love and knows her own value too well, and perhaps she has reason on her side. She is beautiful and accomplished, and the man who marries her will get a princess and half a kingdom. There is no knowing how many men are sighing for her. If you want to pity, rather pity those disappointed suitors. If cousin Kusum really did receive a scar from this affair, rest assured it is healed by this time."

" You should not be so quick to judge. Do you not know that they remember longest who do not fall in love easily ? "

" Yes, if my cousin had loved him in any high degree, but don't you fear that she has done that. The man is attractive, he creates a temporary impression on others by his conversation and manners, but I do not see how any one could fall in love with him very deeply. I could not, of that I am certain, and it now appears that you did not either, and yet you think Kusum might have lost her heart."

"You exhibit extraordinary logic."

"We read much in English literature of love at first sight, but, believe me, that means only a slight emotion that inexperienced youth mistakes for love. Now it is just possible that Kusum felt a little bubbling of the heart, but no doubt it has subsided ere this. True love can never be based on mere impulse; that requires a training of the heart and a fit object to rest upon. Yet if I heard of somebody falling in love with the doctor I could understand it. Do you know we joke cousin Kusum about him; he has become their family physician. I suspect he has been tackled."

The blood coursed madly through my veins, my face became flushed, and I feared I would betray myself, but Chanchal did not notice it, her attention was just then attracted in another direction.

"Here you are, coz," she exclaimed. "You will live long. We were just talking about you, and now you have come."

And really there stood Kusum. I had not met her for a long time. She looked greatly changed. Her eyes lacked their usual brilliancy, and the self-conscious smile that was generally on her lips had disappeared. I felt sorry for her, and fearing that she might think me ungracious spoke to her pleasantly and said:

"I am so glad to see you, Kusum, I have not seen you for an age."

Kusum was reserved and she replied:

"I have often thought of calling on you, but I could not somehow or other succeed in doing so, but why did you not call at our place all this time?"

I was somewhat at a loss for a reply, but presently said:

"I am going home shortly. I have been busy."

"Going into the wilderness in her grief," interrupted Chanchal.

That was ungracious of Chanchal. What would Kusum think of me? She herself seemed to realise that she had said the wrong thing; she, therefore, changed the subject, and asked Kusum about the doctor.

Kusum replied sharply:—

"What do I know of him? Perhaps Moni can tell you, he comes to her house often enough. Why should she grieve about any one? Others would consider themselves lucky if they had her good fortune."

Her object was to vent her feelings on me, but she let out the truth at the same time. As she spoke she sighed, and jealousy and despair shone out of her eyes. It was plain—Kusum had fallen in love, but the question remained with whom—with Romanath or with the doctor?

CHAPTER XVI

CHAPTER XVI

THERE could no longer be any doubt about it that Kusum loved the doctor. Chanchal was only surmising, she did not know how the matter stood. It was evident that Kusum had broken off the engagement with Romanath herself; why should he have objected to so favourable a match?

As long as there is no moonlight the stars appear bright enough, but let the moon come and the stars grow dim. Kusum might have admired Romanath as long as she did not know the doctor, but it was evident now that she had become attached to the latter, otherwise why should she have become so flurried at the mere mention of his name? Poor Romanath, how sorry I felt for him!

Thus through the long hours of the night these thoughts passed through my brain. How fortunate Kusum was. Was I getting jealous of her? Perhaps. People say there is always a certain amount of jealousy in love. Could I consider myself of a different mould from women generally? Jealousy, if such it was, impressed me as a very harmless feeling, it died away in a sigh, it left no malice behind it. How could I indeed allow such a feeling to spring up, for surely Kusum was not guilty of any wrong, she had not robbed me of anything? What I never possessed could not be taken from me. If he loved her, it was through her own deserts, and if he did not love her, it did not necessarily follow that he should bestow his love on me. The strangest part of it all was, that I began to love Kusum, for whom I had not so far cherished even friendship. The feeling became so strong, I felt I must draw her towards me, and acting on the impulse I rose from my bed with the intention of writing to her, but as I sat down at my desk I thought better of it. What would Kusum think of me? How absurd I would appear in her eyes.

When my sister saw me the next morning she addressed me cheerfully,

"Do you know that he is coming here?"

My heart began to beat rapidly. "When?" I asked.

"To-morrow, to the tennis party. You

do not speak of your sorrow, but the way in which you are getting more emaciated every day brings the tears to my eyes."

I became embarrassed, so even my sister had noticed it.

"Becoming emaciated! That is all nonsense."

"Why do you grieve so," replied my sister, "over a trifling mistake?"

I started, it was clear she was not speaking of the doctor.

My sister continued. "There is no doubt about the fact that he loves you. He met my husband the other day and himself broached the subject. He said he was mortified by your behaviour, and though there was pressure brought to bear on him from another direction to marry a certain young lady, he had not pledged himself. If you will consent even now he is ready to sacrifice everything. He will come to-morrow, now see that you don't get into a misunderstanding again. You both care for each other, why so much fuss over a little difference?"

My head reeled. I knew it was impossible for me to love him. Then marry him—never. I calmly replied:

"He will have to make no sacrifice on my

account. Why have you renewed this affair? I cannot marry him."

"You are too fastidious about a word," replied my sister. "Just because he has used the word 'sacrifice' you take offence."

"You are mistaken, sister, I have taken no offence. I do not love him, and I do not think he loves me. Why should I accept a sacrifice from one for whom I do not care? If he did, he would not speak of sacrifice."

My sister laughed and said,

"I cannot overcome your argument, Moni, but he will come to-morrow, and he will be able to meet your logic and soothe your troubled feelings."

I saw she did not understand me yet, and I therefore tried to explain.

"Didi,* you are really making a mistake. I do not feel offended. On the contrary, I am glad to think that he may have found another. A great responsibility has been taken from me. I always knew I could not love this man, and now I see he does not love me either, and yet I am supposed to be the cause of his unhappiness. It is a wrong way of reasoning."

My sister became annoyed with me again

* Respectful form of addressing elder sister.

"Moni, I have never before seen a girl so selfish as you are. You have a set notion in your mind that he does not love you, and you are holding on to it as if it were a treasure. However, all will be settled to-morrow. Let there be an interview, and then let us know the result."

I tried to remonstrate with my sister, I pleaded with her.

"I cannot see him, sister, believe me, I cannot. No, tell him I am ill.'

"I cannot do that, Moni. My husband has asked him to come, and has given him to understand that you have no further objection to the marriage, and now you say you will not see him. This is really too bad."

"What can I do? If I meet him, I shall only have to say the same thing over again to him. Believe me, Didi, I can never marry this man."

"Do you know that people are already laughing about us? Do you realise what that means to us and to you more particularly? Do you think you are acting wisely?"

"I cannot love him."

"You are an extraordinary girl. Only a few days back you loved him so ardently, and now you declare you can never love him. Never mind, don't give way to foolish notions. Once you are married, you will understand that you do love him."

My sister's persistence drove me almost to despair.

"Sister, I implore you, do not force me to see him. I do not understand everything. I thought for a while that I loved him, but I know better now. If I marry him, two lives will be made miserable."

"Then do exactly as you think best for yourself. I have no more to say. I have never yet seen such an obstinate girl."

And my sister walked away angry and excited to a high degree.

CHAPTER XVII

CHAPTER XVII

I HAVE had many and great struggles in my life, but they have not overpowered me as this one did. I felt as if I were facing a great danger, standing alone in the dark while sharp weapons were aimed at me from every direction. Overcome by anguish, I prostrated my sorrow-stricken soul at the feet of the Divine Mother.

"Oh, Mother of Mercy," I pleaded, "open up the earth before me that I may bury myself therein."

And lo, the Mother took compassion upon me and sent redress, for while I was still praying a servant announced my father's arrival. There was hope, there was light. Father had come to the rescue. He had previously written that he would come, but I had not expected him so soon.

He had gone to my sister's room and I went there to greet him, but when I approached the door, I became so frightened, thinking of what had happened, I dared not go further. From the room came angry voices. My father seemed in a passion of rage and was remonstrating with my sister. I knew that all this was on my account, and remained standing on the threshold. They did not notice me.

"I tell you," I heard my father say, "it is a wonder to me that I have not gone mad over all I have heard. You tell me that Moni herself broke off the engagement, but it is being whispered about that he found the girl wanting in goodness and modesty and therefore refused to marry her. What am I to say to that?"

"It is false," replied my sister emphatically.

"False, of course it's false! How many girls are there that possess the inborn humility and modesty that Moni has."

"Yes, that is true, but I meant even more. Mr. Roy has never said unkind things about Moni. He is even now willing to marry her."

"Willing to marry her! Do you think I will give my daughter to that man?"

"But try and be calm, father, and you will see that all scandal will immediately be averted if she marries him."

"Whatever people may say, whatever scandal and disgrace there may be, it is certain I will never give my child to that wicked man."

"But, father, you do the man injustice, you do not know him. I am certain these reports do not come from him."

But my father's anger was not pacified, he continued as before: "He is a scoundrel. He feels humiliated because our Moni will not marry him, and to save himself he has circulated these reports, and I am to give my girl to him? Never! I will take Moni home with me to-night. I will myself secure a bridegroom for her, one whom I can trust. I want no more of your English courtships."

My sister urged him to remain at least for a day or two, but my father would listen to no entreaties. That very night we left for Dacca. I was happy when I stepped into the train, I felt a burden taken from me. I committed myself entirely to my father's care, and oh, how peaceful it felt, but, alas! I was awakened from my dream too soon; this is a world that envies us repose and peace.

When we were on board the steamer

passing along the river Padma father suddenly said:

"Do you remember Chotu?"

"Yes, father, I do."

"His mother wishes to make you her daughter-in-law, and I, too, would like to take Chotu as my son. It is not every day such a desirable bridegroom is to be had. If fortune favours us, we will celebrate the marriage with as little delay as possible after we arrive at Dacca."

I felt like one struck by lightning. I remembered the time when being married to Chotu was the one vision of my youthful life, but now!

CHAPTER XVIII

CHAPTER XVIII

No sooner had I crossed the threshold of my father's house, than my aunt accosted me.

"Good Heavens, what a big girl, and not married! What will people say when they see her? How can we eat our rice and have that girl on our hands."

My father appeared nervous and tried to make excuses.

"She will not be unmarried much longer. Everything has been settled, as you know. So don't get excited."

His words were barely audible, and he seemed to be anxious to get away, but my aunt was fretting still. She continued:

"Indeed, yes, why should I worry? It is all very well to talk, but people will come to see her, and what will they say when they see such a big girl unmarried? It will not be you then who will have to listen to it all, it will be I who will have to reply to it."

Poor aunt! she had indeed cause for

anxiety. No sooner had the news spread about that I had come home, than there were visitors by the dozen. It seemed as if the whole female population of the town had turned out to greet me. Relations, friends, neighbours, every one knew me and had a claim upon me, and the burden of their song was ever the same!

"What! such a big girl and not married! How can you eat your rice, how can you sleep at night?" etc., etc. The condemnation fell upon my father and every one went away with the satisfaction of having said something sharp about him. He had neglected his duty as a father, he had sinned against Society. He had a nineteen-year-old spinster on his hands, and that was an unpardonable offence.

Aunt forgot her grief over my sad lot by joining the chorus. She, too, began to blame my father and seemed to take a morbid delight in doing so. My condition in the face of all this can be understood. My life became well-nigh unbearable. Still I felt resolved on one point—it would be far better for me to remain unmarried and continue being worried than to be joined to a man for whom my heart cared not. The whole affair put a severe strain upon me, under which my nervous system threatened to break down.

These things continued to be of daily recurrence—the unsparing criticism of the people, aunt's admonitions to my father, his assurance that all would be well in the end; but I heard no more of any settled marriage, nor was Chotu mentioned to me again. So notwithstanding the fact that my heart was by no means entirely at ease, I became more composed daily. Trepidation left me and I gradually became so calm that I could take a reasonable view of what was going on around me. If people said unkind things, it was because they could not overcome time-honoured custom, I argued, and instead of being annoyed with them any longer, I began to respect them for the strength of their convictions.

Suddenly my palace of calm was broken to pieces again, for father took me by surprise one day during dinner; he announced:

"Chotu will be here in a day or two. The date of the marriage will be fixed as soon as he comes."

This was good news for aunt. She ejaculated with delight:

"The bridegroom is himself coming! I thought his mother was coming first. But never mind that, times are changing and nowadays a young man must see his bride before marrying her. Let him see her then, that does not matter, but no further delays. The marriage must take place this month and no later."

My father agreed with her.

"That too is my wish," he replied.

CHAPTER XIX

CHAPTER XIX

I DID not know what happened to me after this information, my mind was in a turmoil. After dinner father went to the outer apartment and I was left to think over my fate. Suddenly I felt myself growing strong, my natural shyness left me, and I entered my room still confused, yet with a strong determination. I would let my father know how I felt. I could not face him and explain, but I could write, and write I did.

"To your honoured feet,

"Dear Father,

I have no desire to marry. I have examined my heart carefully, and I know I shall find no happiness in marriage. Do not therefore think my resolution is the result of a foolish fancy. I hear that in England many a girl remains unmarried and spends her life in service to her country. Grant me to do likewise, let me dedicate my life in service to the Motherland. There alone will I find happiness. Do not, I beseech you, dear father, make me unhappy by urging me into marriage.

"Your loving daughter,

"MRINALINI."

I sent a servant with the letter to father, taking care that it should reach him before he went out again. I waited for a reply with anxious and palpitating heart. Presently I heard footsteps, my father was coming. Suddenly my shyness returned and I thought I could not show him my face again. He entered the room and remained standing in one spot. I felt his gaze upon me although I stood with my head bent down. After a pause he spoke:

"I see you have a very mistaken idea about marriage. Must you necessarily remain single in order to serve your country? Even if you did, you could not do much in that direction under the present conditions. You will be able to fulfil the duties of your life far better married than single, and I have not the least doubt that you will be happy. For both the temporal and spiritual well-being of woman marriage is the best road. You are only a child and know nothing of life. If I acted upon your advice I would prepare unhappiness for you. It is my regret that I have not been able to marry you before now, but fortunately I have succeeded in securing a good bridegroom in the end. Thank God for this blessing and be prepared to receive your husband with a joyful heart."

My father did not wait for a reply but left me abruptly. His determination was firm, I was powerless. I realised I could not disobey him. I was after all but a weak Bengali girl; I could but obey. There was no alternative. I could not after this speak further to my father, so I had to face the inevitable.

CHAPTER XX

CHAPTER XX

As it began to dawn upon me more and more that there was no escaping, thoughts crowded my brain in mad confusion. I saw not the world that surrounded me, I was hardly aware of time and space, my mind had entered a dreamy state. At intervals I felt a sensation of acute pain, a desire to see light through the darkness that enshrouded me. At these moments I felt like one maddened by a keen struggle to break through chains that are too strong to be broken. It seemed like irony that of all men Chotu should be the cause of all this, Chotu whom I had loved so much, upon whom I had looked as a friend. Then suddenly a thought dawned upon me, it came like a revelation: Chotu, the friend of my childhood, whom I had trusted as never another, Chotu was to be my saviour now. To him I would explain everything and he would come to my rescue. Now my mental atmosphere became clear once more.

I felt like one giddy with joy at the inspiration that had taken hold of me. Yes, Chotu would save me.

While still I was reflecting upon all that might or might not be, a servant came and handed me a card. What strange accident of fate was this? The doctor! my heart stood almost still; it was not joy that caused it, but amazement. I was like one in a trance when I told the servant to show him in. I was alone in the drawing-room, the only private apartment the house afforded. I had fled thither to be away from the curiosity and annoying remarks of friends.

Oh, that I knew what was the right thing for me to do. Was it then really proper that I should receive him? It was useless, however, for me to weigh the question further, for before me stood the doctor ere I had time for serious reflection.

"You appear very poorly, are you suffering still?" He said this almost immediately after entering.

I do not know whether there was the expression of any deep sympathy in these words, but they affected me deeply. It required great effort to suppress my tears and I could falter only a few words in reply.

"You here? How did you come?" He seemed surprised. "Did you not know I would come? I wrote to Mr. Mazumdar (my father) that I would be here to-day."

My father was not in the habit of communicating all his affairs to me. I therefore replied, "No, I had not heard of it. You have perhaps come here in connection with a case."

He remained silent for a while, then said:

"I have come here expressly to see you. I had no other object in coming."

This was a great surprise to me, he had come expressly to see me! On the impulse of the moment I cried out:

"That is really extraordinary; you did not seem so eager to see me in Calcutta."

He smiled and fixed his clear, full gaze upon me.

"I see I made one of my many mistakes in acting as I did, but did you not understand me? Did you not feel why it was I came so seldom?"

"How could I understand?"

He adjusted his eyeglasses, he was evidently a little nervous, then he looked at me with that sweet, tender look that I had seen in his eyes when he leaned over me as I woke from my deep faint.

"I remained away only to control my desire to come again and again," he whispered.

"Then am I to understand that because you have come now, you wish never to come again?"

"That would be making a mistake again," he replied, smiling sadly, and then as I did not speak, after a pause he began again:

"Circumstances have changed since I first met you. You were then engaged to be married. That is all over now, that is why——"

Again he was silent, while I stood with throbbing heart, the perspiration breaking out upon my forehead. Was it really true? What did all this mean? He continued:

"That is why I have come to offer you my life, my soul, my being—the decision lies with you."

Can language describe the moments that followed? I felt myself lifted to the realms of ecstasy. All existence seemed merged into that moment. He was mine, mine, my heart throbbed, my head reeled, I could not grasp it. If there be Heaven on earth it came to me that minute when he offered his life to me, but alas! this great earth of ours holds the reality of Heaven but a second and then appears more threatening than ever. I felt as if by some mocking phantom I had been led to the gates of Paradise, there to bid farewell to it for ever.

Seeing I did not answer, he spoke again:

"Have you nothing to say to me? Ever since the day I saw you after my return from abroad, I have known that I love you, that without you my life will be empty."

I interrupted him. "But you are engaged."

"Am I? I did not know it. Where did you hear that?"

"I understand your mother herself said so."

He laughed and replied,

"My mother said so! Well, I am not surprised to hear that. Whenever my mother sees a girl who appears good-looking to her she makes up her mind that that very girl must become her daughter-in-law. If polygamy were still in vogue, she would have had half a dozen daughters-in-law by this time. Don't let that disturb you further. I am asking for a reply to my appeal."

What could I say? Was I not his, body and soul? How could I tell him that I was to become the wife of another? At last I replied timidly, hardly knowing myself how I came to say it:

"I am engaged. Father has already settled my marriage."

How strangely sad he looked, how strangely still the room seemed, for neither of us dared to speak after that for a long time.

I saw the struggle that went on within him. At last he spoke, but his voice was barely audible.

"What made Mr. Mazumdar behave in this way? However, let that pass, it should be discussed with him. I ask you only to reply to one question. Do you wish to marry the man your father has selected for you?"

All at once I lost my shyness, I lifted my head high and looked into his eyes as I spoke.

"No, I do not wish it. I have loved you

since the day I met you first, and I shall never love another."

I saw his face change all of a sudden, he looked like one inspired, and when he spoke again his voice was sweet and mellow.

"Have you told your father this?"

I was surprised at his question. "How can I say this to my father?" I replied. "I only told him that I wished to remain unmarried, that marriage would not make me happy."

"And his reply?"

"He told me I must marry. Poor father, how can I disobey him? Is it not my duty to make him happy?"

"But do you owe no duty to love, do you owe no duty to yourself, nor yet to the man who cannot face life without you? Ought you to sacrifice your life and his to some misconceived idea of duty? I really do not think your father would force you into marriage with another if he once came to know how the matter stands."

I knew that what he said was only too true, but I did not reply until he spoke again, with an air of impatience this time.

"If you cannot speak to your father, let me do so."

"No, no, do not speak to my father. Listen, I have a plan. The man to whom my father has betrothed me is a friend of my childhood, Chotu, we called him. I have great faith in him. I know Chotu will save me. I loved him when I was a little girl, and I regard him still as a dear friend. The thought of him fills me with happy memories, but I cannot give him my heart. I am certain Chotu would never wish me to be unhappy, I know him too well for that."

"Chotu ?" he exclaimed, "you are to be married to Chotu ? Certainly, if he has any manliness in him, he will help you."

He almost laughed out loud as he said this. I could not understand him and enquired :

"Do you know Chotu ?"

He did not reply to my question. It seemed he did not hear it. He only said :

"This is a world of illusions. Well, tell Chotu and let me know the result. I am off. I may come back this evening, but if I do not come until to-morrow, do not take it amiss. I have not seen your father yet."

And he departed—rather abruptly I thought, not allowing me to say a word in reply.

CHAPTER XXI

CHAPTER XXI

Happiness at last, my father willing, but the doctor had not come and I could not communicate the good news to him. It was a moonlight night, and I seated myself in the garden, anxiously looking down the road. He was coming now, and I went to meet him. By the time I reached the road, however, he had gone so far ahead, he saw me not. I followed him, but lost sight of him at a turning. I became anxious and climbed up an elevation to see where he had gone. Just then a girl came to me with a flower basket in her hand. It was Prabha, a friend of my early life who had been one of my little schoolmates at Babu Krishna Mohan's school. I greeted her, and she replied, "When did you come? I only arrived myself to-day. I plucked these flowers for you and wish to present them to you now."

I answered, "I am in a difficulty. I wish to speak to *him*, but cannot find him."

"Come to my place," she said.

Then her younger brother came along on horseback. Prabha asked,

"Do you know where the doctor is?"

"Yes, I do," came the reply. "If you will mount my horse, Moni, I will show you where he is."

I mounted the horse and it ran off like lightning. It ascended a high rocky plain. I tried to check it, but it flew on like *Pakshiraja.* I thought I should fall to the ground. Then a camel came down the road. The driver saw my danger and jumped down to stop my horse, but it had already stopped. I got down. It was dark now, night had come, and I found myself in an unknown and desolate place. I could not return home because I could not find my way. I walked up the road, but it became narrower and narrower as I proceeded, and there were high walls of earth on either side of it. At the end of the lane there was a small cottage. I entered it. In it was an old lady with a calm, sweet face. She spoke to me and bade me enter: "Come in, little mother, come. Where are you going? Come and sit down."

"I have lost my way," I replied, but she did not seem to hear me.

"Come and sit down and take a little coffee," she continued. "Do you see my garden in front of the house? I planted coffee there with my own hands."

A lamp was burning in the room. Ornaments and garments were scattered on the floor around the lamp.

"Why are these things lying here?" I questioned.

"She has gone away. She promised to come back; so far she has not come, but she will be here presently."

"Who?"

"My daughter-in-law; she is beautiful as the golden moon."

I saw she was a maniac. She had lost her daughter-in-law, and now she awaited her return, keeping her ornaments and garments scattered in the room with her. I felt sad to see all this, and my eyes filled with tears.

The old lady continued, "Mother, who are you? Are you my daughter-in-law? Have you come at last? He has gone into exile, and has not yet returned."

My heart felt as if it were breaking, and

tears flowed from my eyes. And then I awoke and found myself still weeping. I looked at my watch. Scarcely half-an-hour had elapsed since the doctor's departure, and I might not have slept more than five minutes, but the heavy load of despair that had weighed on my mind before I went to sleep had awakened with me. I was as sad as ever. I stood by the window pondering over the fate that was before me. If I told Chotu everything in the hope that he would rescue me, might I not find myself mistaken ? He might not after all be the good man I supposed him to be. In reality I did not know anything about him. Perhaps Chotu loved me still and would insist on marrying me. My heart felt doubly sad as this thought suggested itself. I looked up to the sky in supplication, I pleaded with the Divine Mother to save me. It was the time of sunset, the clouds were gloriously tinted, and a magnificent spectacle it was to see the great masses of cloud, overspread with all the colours of the rainbow, ever changing as the moments passed ; rose, violet, yellow, green, and crimson softly mingling their shades until the heavens appeared like a coloured mountain range.

Red clouds bordered with blue and white shaded with black, grey softly tinged with rose, an exquisite blending of each colour with another.

One colour ever shaded with another, "Yes, such," I murmured, "are the ways of this world, never a smile without a tear, no happiness without an equal portion of sorrow. I wish some God would change this law, and make mankind happier." And yet why should I lament? What was I after all but an atom in the great ocean of life?

I found myself seated at the piano before I knew it. I began to play unconsciously, I knew not why, the song that was so near my heart:

> Alas, we met
> When moon and stars had faded,
> Spring-time had fled and flowers withered lay.
> Garland in hand through the dark night I awaited
> The bridegroom who would come when all was bright and gay.
> Then the house would be filled with fragrance and soft music,
> And the mellow flute the tune of Sahana would play."[1]

This was all I knew of the song, and I sang it over and over again. Suddenly, I heard some one singing behind me, finishing the song :

" Alas, it came, the longed-for moment auspicious,
But I saw him not then, for heavy with sleep were my eyes.
I wreathed not his brow at the moment the gods had selected.
I woke from my sleep, and lo, dark and cold were the skies,
And faded the wreath. I hung on his neck the dead garland,
While my heart throbbed with pain and heavy my bosom with sighs.
Alas, we met
When moon and stars had faded,
Spring-time had fled and flowers withered lay."[1]

The music sent a magic feeling through my being. I was absorbed by it. I looked not at the singer, but played till the sweet song was finished. When at last I did look there came upon me again that strange sensation when the past was merged in the present and the present in the past, when childhood and youth were blended, and I knew myself only as the little girl who had learned to love Chotu when he taught her at his uncle's *Patshala*. Was it really he ? " Are you Chotu, are you Chotu ? " Once again these words come to my lips, but, alas ! again as before to remain unspoken.

I heard footsteps—my father was coming. I rose to greet him and stood still with bashfulness. My father entered and called out cheerfully, "Ah, you, Binoy Krishna! Moni, do you not recognise him? He is Chotu."

Was I dreaming still? Could this be eally true?

CONCLUSION

CONCLUSION

THAT evening as I looked upwards I saw another sky. There were the same clouds, the same vibrating colours of sunset, but all breathed peace and happiness, there was no sorrow in the whispering breeze that night.

Nor was I alone as my gaze went heavenward that night, and the inward cry that this earth knows no happiness, no smile without tears, that cry that had haunted me so long was stilled at last. We were sitting together, Chotu and I, silently absorbed in the love of our young lives. To me the shading of the clouds had another message now. "Smiles," they whispered, "would not be so precious if they had not known tears, happiness would not know itself if it were not born of suffering." Did he think as I did, for suddenly he gave expression to my silent thoughts and said—

"Happiness is not happy enough, but must grow by the contact of pain and fear."

Too much happiness made me sigh, and with it came the pain of remorse. Poor Romanath, if he had really loved me, I had done him grave injustice. Chotu seemed to feel my thoughts. He spoke somewhat abruptly, saying :

"Have you heard the latest news? Kusum is to be married to Romanath. What a humbug—I beg your pardon—what an exemplary lover!"

I was delighted, and interrupted him in my eagerness to hear more.

"Really? When?"

"A week before our marriage?"

The light of the newly risen moon fell upon his handsome face as he spoke, and I thought I had never before seen him look so beautiful. The moon of the thirteenth lunar day, that wanted but two digits to make it full, how glorious it was! It floated like a mellow silver orb in the deep blue ocean of ether. The fragrant *Sephalica* fell around us like a rain of meteorites, and the air was filled with beauty and fragrance. The autumn air was mellow and soft, and it flowed into our being, and all was love and beauty.

It was I who broke the silent spell.

"But you, doctor, how could you?"

"Doctor again?—I will not listen."

"But how could you, Chotu, cause me so much pain? When you understood from my remarks that father had settled my marriage with you, that very moment you left me alone."

"Yes, it appeared from what you said that I was the man, but I was not certain. There might have been a mistake. Love gets easily frightened."

"Was that the reason you left me to my misery? Is that your idea of chivalry?"

"But don't you see, I intended to come back without delay. I wished only to speak to your father, and then Binoy Krishna would present himself before you as Chotu."

"No doubt, that would have been charmingly romantic, but had you no thought of the misery that I underwent in the meantime? So that was the extent of your love?"

He laughed and replied:

"And the extent of your love, my lady? You did not even recognise me, and yet I knew you the first minute I saw you."

"Oh, that is small wonder. The minute you came to the house you knew all about me, and then you kept your identity concealed. You did not even care to speak to me of bygone days. I don't think you loved me so very deeply."

"Now, listen. Was I not told that the lady of my heart was betrothed to another? When I found she did not even recognise me, I thought it wise not to make myself known to her. You do not love Chotu, the friend of your childhood, you love the new man, the doctor."

"And you do not love me, you love the companion of your childhood."

I thought at one time that individuality disappeared in love, and that love was all self-abnegation, but now I find that as light and shade are both required for a landscape, so altercations and demands are also adjuncts of love, and in this way love is kept ever young.

At any rate in our lives love is full of challenge. "You do not love me," I say mockingly, "you love the companion of your childhood."

"You do not love me," is the inevitable reply. "You love the man you met at your sister's house, the doctor."

And now I leave it to the judgment of the

reader to decide whom I have loved. Did I love the companion of my childhood and perceive the reflection of him in the doctor whom I met again as a man and a stranger, or did I love the man, and obtain the companion of my childhood by accident? I love, I admit, but the question remains, "Whom?"